INSPIRATION

Inspiration

Capturing the Creative Potential of Your Organisation

Nicholas Ind
Cameron Watt

palgrave
macmillan

First published 2004 by
PALGRAVE MACMILLAN
Houndmills, Basingstoke, Hampshire RG21 6XS and
175 Fifth Avenue, New York, N.Y. 10010
Companies and representatives throughout the world

PALGRAVE MACMILLAN is the global academic imprint of the Palgrave Macmillan division of St. Martin's Press, LLC and of Palgrave Macmillan Ltd. Macmillan® is a registered trademark in the United States, United Kingdom and other countries. Palgrave is a registered trademark in the European Union and other countries.

ISBN 1–4039–2058–3

This book is printed on paper suitable for recycling and made from fully managed and sustained forest sources.

A catalogue record for this book is available from the British Library.

A catalog record for this book is available from the Library of Congress.

10 9 8 7 6 5 4 3 2 1
13 12 11 10 09 08 07 06 05 04

Printed and bound in Great Britain by
Creative Print & Design (Wales), Ebbw Vale

Contents

List of Figures

Preface

The American literary critic, Harold Bloom (2001), wrote an engaging book called *How to Read and Why* in which he argues that the value of reading is that it helps us to form our own opinions. Yet much business literature is dogmatic. It believes in causality; in one right way. We don't buy into that. Our approach is based on Sir Francis Bacon's premise about reading, which Bloom quotes:

> read not to contradict and confute, nor to believe and take for granted, nor to find talk and discourse, but to weigh and consider. *(p21)*

Our aim with *Inspiration* is to share the results of our research about creativity and to provide examples of organisations that are truly inspirational. We hope that it will help you to reflect on the creative status of your organisation and encourage you to think about how you can emulate the creativity of the businesses in this book such as Quiksilver and Aardman Animations. However, you will have to do it within the cultural context of your own organisation, so the lessons we cite will have to be adapted: you will have to 'weigh and consider' the implications. To help this process we have constructed this book in a series of linked chapters. The first chapter of each pair, sets out the key arguments of a particular theme of creativity, while the second brings the theme to life through specific examples. Thus Chapter 2 looks at the themes of culture and structure, while Chapter 3 features the themes within the context of different organisations: in this case three design consultancies, IDEO, Gensler and Design Bridge. Of course, the chapters are not hermetically sealed. There are some crossovers – IDEO is quoted also in other chapters, because its arguments extend beyond structure and culture – but there is always a clear connection between the theme and the example.

Having read (or indeed while reading) *Inspiration*, you may become hungry for more information or the visual stimuli of powerful images. To help with this, we have constructed a website to inspire you: www.inspiration-book.com It features further information about the book, the featured organisations and photographs. It adds an extra dimension to reading. We hope you enjoy the book and the website.

NICHOLAS IND
CAMERON WATT

Acknowledgements

Our thanks to Randy Hild, Natas Kaupas and Andrea Feldberg of Quiksilver, Sara Öhrvall of Ninety, Lars Nittve of Moderna Museet, Tim Brown of IDEO, Ed Friedrichs of Gensler, Gaute Godager of Funcom, Kerstin Nilsson of the IceHotel, Jill Marshall, Andrea Paul, Carol Destre and all the staff at Design Bridge, Baback Yazdani of Premier Auto Group, David Pickard of Glyndebourne Opera, David Sproxton and Miles Bullough of Aardman Animations, Mairi Macintyre of Warwick Manufacturing Group, Peter Lynam of British Airways, Bryan Brown and all the staff at Marketplace Design and Johan Wistrand and all at Summer for the design and development of the book's web site.

The authors would also like to thank Sage Publications, Inc. for permission to reproduce an adaptation of Morgan's hybrid spider plant model (Figure 6.2).

Inspiration and Creativity

Introduction

Think of something that inspires you. It could be the scale and spectacle of the Bilbao Guggenheim, the visual appeal of a Bang and Olufsen hi-fi, the highly personalised service of the US retailer Nordstrom or the indulgence of a meal at London's Bibendum restaurant. Now think what that sense of inspiration does to you. It should excite you, make you feel special and give you a sense of real engagement. This is why creativity is important. It creates a point of difference and builds a bond between a brand and its customers. But just think how often you're inspired by your relationship with a brand. Probably not as often as you would like. The few positive experiences stand out like a beacon for most of us. This raises the question of why we don't have more inspired experiences. That is part of the quest of this book: to understand the processes that enable creative and inspired organisations to be innovative (and to understand the barriers that prevent others). Our argument, based on more than five years of research among highly creative businesses, emphasises the fact that organisational creativity is the result not of exceptional individuals (although they can often be important inspirers and influencers) but of exceptional groups. This simple change of perspective turns on its head much of the thinking of the personal creativity industry. Our goal is to help make the organisation itself more creative. In doing so we tackle three core issues:

■ What are the key forces and relationships that affect creativity?

■ What role does trust play in enabling people to be creative?

■ How can managers help build cultures that stimulate creative behaviour?

To understand the workings of creativity we chose to study businesses where the idea of creativity is an inherent part of the culture. Our interest was to find out not why these organisations had the occasional creative idea, but how they maintain a competitive advantage through continuous creativity. Examples such as Aardman Animations, Glyndebourne Opera Company, Premier Automotive Group, IDEO, Quiksilver, Sony, Tate Modern and Funcom have informed the development of our ideas. From interviews with managers and staff at these and other significantly creative companies we have been able to build up an understanding of best creative practice. To inspire you, the examples have been crafted into a series of narrative chapters that are designed to illustrate the creativity management models we have developed which will help you manage these complex but fundamental phenomena.

Creativity and competitive advantage

As the globalisation of markets continues and competition increases, the value of creativity in generating significant advantage becomes clear. First, creativity offers tangible differentiation through the delivery of original and valuable products, services and business solutions. Today very few organisations offer customers anything truly different. Pick an industry sector such as fashion, automotive or financial services, or even your own industry, and ask yourself where is the real, significant, tangible difference between one brand and another. Put aside clever marketing techniques and go to the heart of what is on offer. In most cases you will find little if any significant differentiation. Companies are inherently risk averse because of the pressure to deliver ongoing performance. As competition increases so does risk aversion. Managers look to their near competition for ideas or rely on dry, general, abstracted research that, more often than not, encourages mediocre incremental change. One confectionery company introduces foil wrappers or bite-sized product variations and everyone else follows, too scared or creatively limited to do anything else. As a result of such action, business-to-business customers and retail consumers are faced with a plethora of me-too products and services. In today's cash-rich, time-poor society we are desperate for products that clearly offer us something new, exciting and beneficial and we are willing to pay a premium for the pleasure. Originality in itself is attractive to many, but if you attach real buyer benefits, your competitive situation becomes unbelievably strong. Think of Dyson, Apple, Sony, 3M or easyJet – each has gained competitive advantage through innovation. Their creativity clearly positions them in our mind.

Second, being a creative organisation strengthens image and reputation by association with such desirable attributes as energy, knowledge, flair, motivation and the ability to offer something new and valuable. Creativity is desirable, sexy and exciting. Creative organisations employ the best and brightest and they provide products and services to the successful and enlightened. Having a brand that is perceived as creative attaches these sorts of emotional attributes to it. Your brand becomes seen as the leader, the solution finder, the best.

Finally, creative organisations exhibit strong internal commitment and cooperation; they support the intrinsic needs of their staff and help develop shared values and visions. Such environments not only increase employee motivation, but also compound organisational knowledge by facilitating open communication and maintaining low staff turnover. Too often managers forget the value of employee creativity in their organisations. People who work for creative brands love their work. They want to stay and continue having fun, to be challenged and to produce products and services that they feel are exciting and valuable. They are truly committed to the brand vision and will live it in everything they do.

Organisations can no longer see creativity as being pertinent to only artistic or entrepreneurial companies, nor can it be viewed as a mysterious or fringe subject. Creativity needs to exist as a core construct of any organisation wishing to compete effectively.

The Van Gogh paradox

There are numerous books, articles and academic papers that discuss the nature of creativity. Do not panic, we have no intention of entering into a deep theoretical debate about the meaning of creativity – such intellectual discussion can be left for another time. Intuitively, we all know what creativity is. We have experienced it on many occasions in films, plays, books, paintings and perhaps occasionally as consumers. Probably the one place we rarely experience it is at work. We recognise creativity when it happens, yet few of us try to decode how or why something is creative. For us (and most people) creativity is about new ideas or new ways of seeing things. However, placing creativity in a commercial context complicates things slightly. There is no doubt in our minds that Van Gogh was a creative genius, but he only sold one painting in his lifetime; Leonardo da Vinci's greatest ideas never saw the light of day and are only appreciated from today's perspective. At the time people did not place a value on his ideas. In some cases they were too short-sighted, while in others the ideas were so advanced they had no meaning to people at that time or could not be implemented due to limited resources or knowledge.[1] Commercial reality is about gaining competitive advantage and increasing shareholder value. Ideas have to be seen to have some sort of value or the potential to deliver benefits. If that value is not deemed to exist or benefits are not evident the idea may just be new and not relevantly creative.

In judging the creativity of an idea we face a dilemma – the Van Gogh paradox. If, as managers, we do not perceive an idea as having value, is the idea poor or are we merely limited by lack of imagination, market intuition or fear of failure? What can we do to prevent ideas being lost? How can we nurture ideas that are not right for now but could be in the future? How do we ensure ideas keep coming from all quarters of the organisation? How do we ensure opportunities are taken and serious mistakes not made? The only thing that is certain is that we can never get it right all the time. As managers you could have a Van Gogh in your hands and not see it. The key is to limit the times this happens, increase creative recognition, develop nurturing systems and encourage staff to produce more and more ideas of such quality that you and they begin to see their commercial potential at an instinctive level. This book will help you develop and maintain such an environment.

Creativity is a collective act

A great deal of early research into creativity focused on the individual within an educational or military context. It was believed that the results of such work would not only increase our understanding of what makes people creative but also help to predict and develop the creative potential of individuals. In more recent years this work has entered the area of management research. The early focus, made famous by such writers as Edward de Bono (1967) and Tudor Rickards (1988), was on individual training and development techniques aimed at maximising creative thinking. The basis of this work is the belief that everyone has the ability to be more creative and that this can be achieved through the use of personal training techniques such as brainstorming, mind mapping and lateral thinking. The problem is that this work does not place creativity within a social context but remains fixed on the individual. There is little attempt made to examine how external factors influence the person or process. Instead, the researchers limit their investigations to cognitive approaches based on left brain/right brain theories. But, creativity does not occur in isolation. Even though ideas come from individuals, the antecedents of those ideas are the result of social interaction between any number of people and situations. Ivory towers do not exist.

Although training can be useful in both aiding personal ability and communicating senior management commitment through resource allocation, it will not facilitate creativity by itself. Before any such training can be effective, the environments within which people interact and exist need to become conducive or responsive to such thinking. Moreover the dynamic relationships that are part of the process need to be understood and managed. Relying on individually focused work assumes that either the social environment does not have significant impact or that the environment is already responsive and well managed. To encourage genuine creativity you need to sow seeds on fertile ground and then ensure they are watered for germination to occur. To continue this horticultural analogy, you also have to keep up a constant cycle of maintenance and nurturing. We believe that managers need to shift their focus away from creative-thinking training programmes and begin to focus on understanding and managing the complex interactions that occur between people and their context. In other words organisations need to consider and deal with both individual and contextual factors if creativity at work is to be increased.

In this book we emphasise behaviourally focused issues, such as leadership style, communication systems, culture, knowledge, social frameworks and team dynamics. In addition we bring social context into perspective and illustrate the interconnected nature of the process by explaining the underlying personal and interactive relationships that create the dynamic that facilitates creative behaviour. We believe that organisational culture is critical to the creative process as it defines people's perceptions of trust, safety and risk taking. Such perceptions affect the willingness of organisational members to explore and experiment with new ideas or approaches. Essentially, culture, structures and systems provide the social frameworks that either promote or hinder creativity and as such managers need to understand how to manage these contexts if they are to develop and maintain creative environments.

Chapter outlines

Essentially we have broken the book into two distinct yet interconnected parts: narratives on some of the world's most creative organisations and discussion chapters. The objective is to provide a balance of theoretical discussion and practical application. Many readers have rightly criticised management books as being too academic and unconnected to be of everyday use. By introducing standalone stories we illustrate how managers in highly competitive environments succeed in implementing the strategies we highlight in our discussion chapters. This provides the reader with a strong theoretical foundation as well as practical management tools.

■ *Chapter 2* illustrates how managers can develop creative and trust-based cultures. We highlight which core cultural constructs need to exist as well as their influence on the creative process. The latter part of the chapter develops this discussion further by investigating the impact that organisational structures have on the working environment and how stakeholders perceive them. Fundamental trends and their impact on trust and creativity are assessed. We then go on to consider what structural form is required to facilitate trust and creative behaviour within a commercial context.

■ In *Chapter 3* we look at how three design practices – Design Bridge, IDEO and Gensler – manage creative people and environments. We see how deeply embedded cultural beliefs provide vision, clarity and momentum to an organisation and help guide stakeholder behaviour. We also see how culture impacts on relationships and people management as well as creative projects. In addition we examine the value these agencies place on knowledge and how they leverage it to increase their intellectual capital and add value.

■ *Chapter 4* provides key arguments and discussions relating to the abilities and attitudes managers need to possess if they are to manage creative professionals successfully. The concept of senior managers as creative champions is discussed, with the argument being made that such champions should be seen in a group context. The key characteristics of such leaders are highlighted in terms of personality and action, showing how such leadership is critical in building vision and trust. The chapter then introduces the concept of managers as creative mentors and their role as supportive and nurturing leaders who can understand employees' needs and aspirations and challenge and develop their abilities. We go on to highlight key requirements and strategies for motivating and managing creative professionals, arguing that managers need to build and show high levels of trust if they are to manage successfully. Finally, the chapter concludes by arguing that managers may need to pursue the development of much wider and diverse learning networks if they are to facilitate lively debate and idea generation.

■ In *Chapter 5* we have a rare view into the world of animation and game design. Aardman Animations and Funcom sit at the pinnacle of their industries and represent the extreme end of commercial creativity. We investigate how managers in these organisations balance the needs of highly creative and sometimes volatile individuals with those of a commercially driven business. We see that they are able to maintain motivation and focus through delicate application of constraints and frameworks that provide direction and focus yet are flexible enough to ensure creative freedom. Finally we observe the value of emotional intelligence and mentoring in relation to leadership, highlighting their value in developing highly trusting work environments.

■ *Chapter 6* focuses on the tensions occurring within the team dynamic and the effect this has on the creative process. The impact of team structure and role designation is discussed in the context of various parties' perceptions of the working environment and their willingness to act in a benevolent and creative manner. The chapter then proceeds to investigate issues relating to self-organisation, team focus and group diversity. It then moves on to the management of teams, examining how managers can develop a framework that balances the personal and team needs for autonomy and the organisational need for control and commercial objectivity. Finally, we address the issue of interteam conflict, how it arises and what managers can do to maintain equity and energy within a team environment.

■ In *Chapter 7* we focus on how arts organisations such as Glyndebourne and Tate Modern manage creative projects. We discuss the tensions facing such non-profit-making organisations and examine how the attempt to balance social, financial and creative pressures impacts on creativity. The role and structure of teams is seen to be of critical importance when managers realise the value of empowered, knowledgeable and motivated employees. Looking at specific projects we see how a sense of clarity and vision combined with understood responsibilities and boundaries and a deep belief in the organisational brand inspires teams to act creatively.

■ *Chapter 8* reviews the problems facing organisations within the context of customer relations and proposes a series of strategies that companies can adopt in order to facilitate creative relationships. We investigate how organisations can go about developing creative partnerships with stakeholders and focus on how building greater understanding between parties can facilitate a shift in the relationship paradigm to a more trust-based partnership. The chapter emphasises the need for companies to introduce more client-focused frameworks and systems that can balance the need for autonomy with formal processes and communication systems. We argue that such strategies can provide focus and clarity, reduce fear, anxiety and misalignment of expectations, so increasing the potential for trust building, benevolent behaviour and creativity.

■ *Chapter 9* provides a fascinating account of how the clothing and accessories company Quiksilver combines a culture steeped in surfing mythology with the commercial needs of a global company turning over more than $700 million and employing in excess of 3000 people. We see how strongly embedded cultural values based on a surfer's need for personal expression and freedom are balanced with an intrinsic desire to create fresh and exciting product lines that deliver new levels of value to consumers as well as increasing the competitive position of the organisation. We also see how Quiksilver has built on these shared values to develop a networked structure that allows for free-flowing creativity to occur across seemingly traditional organisational and stakeholder boundaries.

■ *Chapter 10* places the brand at the heart of the discussion. After briefly outlining what a brand is, we move on to discuss its value to the creative process in providing direction, focus and vision. Meaningful interaction with the brand provides clarity and inspiration for both internal and external stakeholders and provides a foundation of understanding that helps direct and inform. We argue that brands are valuable in setting boundaries for creativity and for preventing staff from going in the wrong strategic direction but with the caveat that creativity can still stretch a brand and provide it with new meaning. Finally we discuss how the boundaries set by a brand allow for the co-existence of the rational and irrational allowing open debate and questioning to occur in a trusting environment.

■ *Chapter 11* looks at how the creative process is managed in the automotive sector by examining how Ford's Premier Automotive Group and VW-Audi manage projects and develop creative environments. Once again we see how the brand acts as a tool to help in the development of design briefs that are focused, flexible and meaningful. We look at how such briefs are developed and argue that they should be co-created with clients so that they provide creative stimulus rather than technical constraint. A key issue that comes to light is how deep intuitive understanding of customers acts as a spur to creativity and that such understanding does not emerge from traditional market research but from honest engagement and true understanding of the brand.

■ *Chapter 12* provides an opportunity to review the previous chapters and draw out the key findings and their significance in a business context. An overall theory for the management of creative environments, people and processes is put forward, supported by specific practical strategies.

Note

1   Van Gogh's *The Portrait of Dr Gachet* became the most valuable painting ever sold at auction in 1990 when it reached $82.5 million. During his lifetime, one painting was sold – *Red Vineyard*, for 400 francs. Leonardo da Vinci's understanding of the body, technology, aerodynamics and mechanics was only realised some 400 years after his death, primarily because resistance to his ideas at the time was formidable and his work was therefore never published – the Roman Catholic Church believed he was involved in necromancy.

Creative Organisations at Work | 2

Introduction

Creativity is high on the agenda of most managers, yet its realisation is elusive. Such seemingly simple questions as – What is creativity? What can creativity do for our business? How can we be more creative? – create much soul searching. Managers can identify the need to develop new services and ideas but the barriers to achieving them can sometimes appear insurmountable. The tendency is to think this can be resolved by applying tools and techniques: do more brainstorming; more employee engagement schemes; set up independent development teams; change the office space to encourage better interaction. The reality is that these prescriptions are placebos. Tools and techniques work when the culture is supportive. Without context they are simply a veneer.[1] This chapter starts to address some of these basic questions, but does so from a cultural perspective. In so doing, it challenges a number of conventional ideas on personal freedom, the need for organisational boundaries and the role the brand has to play in building and maintaining a creative culture.

Building a creative culture

The essence of creativity is about generating *original* and *valuable* ideas. In these seemingly simple words, lies some complexity. What do 'original' and 'valuable' mean? We might assume that originality is about new-to-the-world ideas, but as Picasso is supposed to have said, 'good artists copy, great artists steal'. As this quotation was used in an interview by Steve Jobs of Apple, we should perhaps also note his idea that creativity is about connecting things. Originality is rarely about completely new-to-the-world thoughts, but is quite often about interesting, and previously unseen, connections.[2] However, for interesting connections to be creative they also need to be valuable.[3] In a business context, that means they have to be relevant, appealing and useful to buyers or other stakeholders. For example, while Sir Clive Sinclair's short-lived C5 single-seater electric vehicle (which was launched in 1985) might have been original, it was not of value to buyers. By way of contrast, the Mercedes/Swatch initiative that led to the Smart car, while perhaps less original as a concept, does provide value to buyers – just try driving round and parking in a crowded European city such as Rome to appreciate the benefit. By our definition the Smart car is a creative idea.

The cultural challenge is to develop more original and valuable ideas and that means confronting the complexity of a social context and the difficulty of managing creativity (with all its risk and uncertainty). This does not mean a Herculean solo effort on the part of the manager, but rather a willingness and ability to engage colleagues with the corporate purpose and to understand the deeper motivations of customers. A powerful example of this is the American department store retailer Nordstrom. This company, which has long harboured a reputation for outstanding customer service, recognises it is primarily the people on the shop floor who determine the customer experience. How Nordstrom achieve excellence is through a focus on recruiting people who like working with other people. Or as Nordstrom say, understatedly, 'we try to hire nice people who want to work hard'. Nordstrom's success is down to a concentration on delivering outstanding customer service and the recognition that the best way to do this is not through a rule book, but through empowering customer-oriented employees. Here, creativity is delivered every day by individual sales people who identify with Nordstrom's purpose. However, Nordstrom is a rarity. Most organisations struggle to overcome the barriers that beset any social environment and impair creativity: egos, fear, poor relationships, lack of ability, lack of empathy and obstinacy.

How then might managers create a social environment that encourages creativity? Managers not only have to lead, but also have to understand their own and their employees' strengths and weaknesses and the subtle relationships that exist throughout their company. They have to understand the cultural needs and to develop a structure that supports creative relationships. Creative cultures are formed in the tensions that exist between the needs and personalities of people and the pressures of commercial environments. This tension creates a volatile dynamic system. On the one hand, traditional management thinking emphasises conformity, control, cost reduction, increased efficiency, consistency, accountability and the need to increase shareholder value. On the other hand is the need to foster cultures that accept and embrace difference, flexibility, freedom of expression, participation, ambiguity, individuality and uncertainty. These seemingly contradictory forces create real problems for today's managers, pushing them far beyond the safety of traditional roles. The challenge is to balance the needs of both forces against one another and create the optimum environmental tensions that stimulate, facilitate debate and inspire creative action, while maintaining operational efficiency.[4]

Start with the right people

One of the findings of Jim Collins' book, *Good to Great*, which analyses the transformation of eleven companies from merely good to great[5] is 'the main point is to first get the right people on the bus (and the wrong people off the bus), before you figure out where to drive it'. Effective creativity needs the right people on the bus, which means managers have to focus on people, their needs, perceptions, expectations, experiences and motivations. It's very hard to develop a creative environment without people who identify with the organisation's ideology and feel they are trusted to experiment and to innovate.

As the example of Nordstrom suggests, getting the personality type right is as important as finding people with the appropriate skills. This is important in two respects. First, by employing people with relevant personality types, the organisation and the individual can match their needs. For example if individuals have a high need to express their individuality, they will probably be ill-suited to a tightly controlled conformist organisation. Equally, a highly innovative organisation probably does not want too many risk-averse people. Yet there are some limits to how far one should take this, which leads us to the second point: some balance between types is needed to prevent group-think. Creativity requires an environment of open dialogue and debate and while a similarity of values and personality type can help build trust, too much can breed complacency. An example of this is provided by the Dutch IT company, Pink Roccade, which, for a time, was so successful at recruiting like-minded people there was no questioning of direction. When the company realised this, it deliberately started to employ some alternative personality types. Similarly Ford's Premier Automotive Group (PAG) actively seeks to insert staff with different personality types into teams or departments that are beginning to exhibit complacency or group-think. As Baback Yazdani, Operations Director, notes:

> We have both personality types here and we have to cleverly position them in the right place. For example if some part of the company is set in its ways you might want to inject someone to shake things up and get people thinking and acting in new ways. If shouting is necessary then shouting we will have. Departments can get ineffective, not inefficient, but not open to new ideas, so we have to get people in to push them around a bit. It's about getting the balance right, knowing what's needed.
>
> *(Interview with author dated 12 August 2003)*

Also, a common theme running through the companies that were researched for this book was that their people shared common beliefs relating to life and work, yet possessed diversity in personal and professional values. For example, having fun, a passion for their field and working hard for their own development, were commonly expressed values but significant differences occurred in terms of preferred working methods, attitudes to customers and the management of projects. The task for managers is to identify and communicate the core values, required skills and experiences and to achieve a productive balance within the workforce.

While placing an emphasis on recruiting the right people, it is also interesting to note that many of the researched companies had largely informal recruitment procedures or competency evaluation frameworks to assist in the selection process. Most followed an ad hoc approach, based on managerial experience and intuition. Key skills are one requirement but personality and a perception that values are shared are as important. The main issue for managers in these firms was whether the candidate would enhance the existing culture. This meant the candidate's personality, attitude and even gender was considered in the context of the culture fit, along with the newness of the skill offered. The process varied but always involved potential recruits being immersed in the culture as much as possible during initial visits.

One question that arises is why the process appears to work so well at some companies and less successfully at others. If we take the UK-based design company Design Bridge as an example, senior managers appear to share the same core personal and work-related values: a sense of fun, integrity and respect for others, as well as a belief in what they do. Second, they understand what those core values are, and have the emotional intelligence to identify them in potential employees. Third, the process is informal and inclusive; it involves a large number of people getting to know applicants in an informal context, allowing them to sense if the personality will fit and whether the skill mix is appropriate.

Although at first this may appear a rather subjective method of selection, when placed in the context of generating trust it becomes understandable. A number of forward-thinking academics and managers have recognised the importance of liking as a basis for trust development (Blois 1999; Cullen et al. 2000; Ford and Gioia 2000; Nicholson et al. 2001). The development of emotional bonds is crucial in building trust, which in turn leads to a reduction in uncertainty and an increase in risk-taking behaviour. Liking an individual, in combination with tangible evidence of ability, increases personal attachment and facilitates trust through the desire to believe that goodwill and integrity exist within that person. If a recruit exhibits useful skills and you and other staff like him, then he is probably the right person. Like all things with creativity, there are no certainties. Sometimes you just have to trust your instincts.

This instinctive approach, which will be further explored in Chapter 9 on Quiksilver, is a cultural phenomenon and seems to occur as a result of a deeply felt connection between the employee and the organisation. This fact emphasises how different organisations can be and how any approach, whether recommended in these pages or other business books, needs to be adaptive to the cultural context. Cultures are driven by, and are representative of, the people within the company. What is deemed a creative culture for one organisation may not be right for another. For example, a culture seen as dynamic, challenging and creative by one group may be perceived as threatening and unsupportive by another. The implication is that managers need to be emotionally intelligent to balance cultural tensions. This requires them to be clear about what sort of company it is, what values are inherent, what strategic objectives and goals exist and what this means in a cultural and creative context. Also, it is important that managers have a clear understanding of their staff in terms of motivation, expectations, needs, aspirations and preferred methods of working. The combination of these abilities enables managers to evaluate their existing culture, develop change strategies and successfully implement them. It is critical that this process be continuous as environments are dynamic and cultural norms are liable to change. If managers are not aware of these fluctuations, cultural strategies can become redundant and run the risk of being perceived as out of touch or uncaring. This in turn leads to poorer internal relationships and reduced creativity.

Create the right balance

There are a number of ideas floating around management circles on how to build and manage cultures. Essentially there are two schools of thought: at one extreme is the belief in individual freedom, at the other is control and regimentation. Our own work, based on the companies highlighted in this book, suggests that the answer lies in developing a middle way, where managers attempt to balance both creative and commercial needs. The logic for balance is straightforward. Too little focus on commercially oriented issues can reduce creativity by limiting a company's ability to manage, think and operate successfully. Lack of structure, systems and business values prevents strong trusting relationships being developed with external stakeholders and confuses internal stakeholders as to strategic direction and behavioural boundaries. Equally, a lack of focus with regard to personal needs and desires reduces intrinsic motivation, commitment and stakeholder cooperation, helping to create a culture of negativity and mistrust.

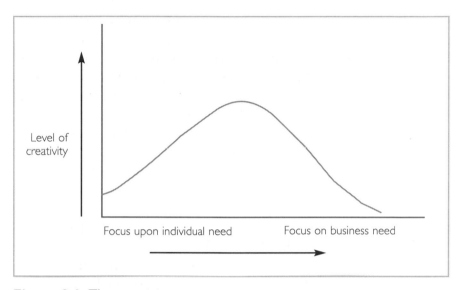

Figure 2.1 The creativity curve

Figure 2.1 provides a simple illustration of this dilemma. It is important to note that the potential level of personal creativity is higher at the personal need end of the spectrum, even though the environment may be highly chaotic and lacking business focus. Original ideas can still be generated here, as the culture will be very open and free. However, the degree of value they are deemed to have in a commercial context will vary considerably as it is unlikely that much strategic input occurs. As Figure 2.1 illustrates, the optimum creativity occurs when the balance between both forces is met.

Although it is dangerous to apply the same cultural model to all organisations, there are certain commonalities, which appear to be core cultural requirements. These provide a social fabric of behavioural, psychological and emotional attributes within which staff exist, form relationships and interact. Each feeds the others, creating an interconnected network of norms that reinforce one another in the minds of employees, generating either a positive or negative cycle of perception. These core factors are trust, enjoyment and fun, valuing creativity, diversity and a desire to learn.

Trust appears at the heart of creative cultures. Without it, openness, experimentation, risk taking, commitment and cooperation are unlikely to occur. In addition, a social, fun-orientated environment, where flexibility, idea generation, communication and relationship development can occur at an informal level, requires trust to exist between people before personal barriers are dropped. Fear is a basic barrier to creativity and occurs in non-trusting environments where self-interest and associated behaviour dominates. In these organisations, people are insufficiently confident to have the courage to try new things or suggest new ideas. Try and use techniques such as brainstorming in this type of environment and there will be a constrained response. Thoughts will not flow freely and the level of creativity will be limited.

It is also valuable to understand the two-way nature of trust in terms of the delivery of promises. How promises are perceived and actioned varies, from implicit understanding of support and integrity, to explicit delivery of outputs; either way it helps form a core part of the trust culture. Managers in our companies seemed particularly aware of this concept, recognising that they had to deliver and fulfil their promises to their staff and organisation. Equally, they felt that the organisation must deliver on its promises, particularly in terms of training, support (professional and personal), breadth of experience and potential for creative expression. When an organisation fails to meet its promises, people become cynical and disillusioned.

Trust feeds into and supports positive values and actions that continue to build as a positive cycle develops. How it manifests itself varies, from definable behaviour such as supportive action, reliability and open communication, to more intangible attributes linked to feelings and climate. Without trust, other attributes of a creative culture would not thrive. Trust and the associated perception of relationship security make it easier to be honest, have fun, develop an open, learning environment, be willing to take on a variety of roles and develop positive relationships. How trust helps to develop a creative culture is illustrated in the trust cycle seen in Figure 2.2. As trust develops and is reinforced, positive beliefs and perceptions increase and are exhibited through creative behaviour, which in turn increases levels of trust within the environment. The process continues in a positive spiral, facilitating creative behaviour, relationships and environments.

It would be easy to ridicule the value of *fun* in a work environment as time wasting or disruptive. However, in a creative context it is essential. Not only does fun help in generating a relaxed, informal

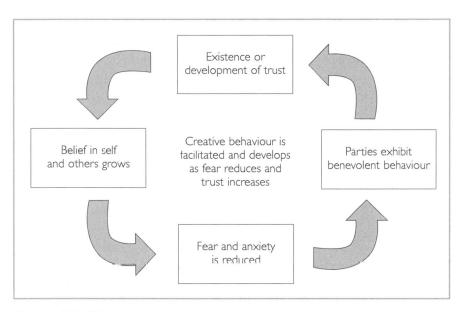

Figure 2.2 The trust cycle

and safe environment, it also helps mental freewheeling by introducing abstract concepts, breaking set patterns of thought and
reducing negative tensions. It is interesting to note, from our own
experiences, how a comical observation often provides an alternative
train of thought from which a valuable idea is generated.

Fun and humour are also valuable in reducing stress and allowing
for moments of down time. Tight deadlines, the competitive nature
of business, the need to generate new ideas again and again and the
personal desire to be creative all help in inducing a stressful environment. Humour acts as a safety valve, allowing staff and managers to
let off steam, take time out and relax for a few precious moments.

Being seen to *value creativity* is important in fostering creative
relationships, as it underpins a core need of staff. If people do not
feel able to express their creativity they will become frustrated and
demotivated. As Abraham Maslow (1998) wrote:

> A musician must make music, an artist must paint, a poet must write, if he is to
> be ultimately at peace with himself. What a man can be, he must be. This need
> we may call self-actualisation. *(p3)*

If senior managers appear to want only safe, straightforward results that will not rock the boat, staff will not see creativity as an option, increasing feelings of ambivalence to projects and the firm. Frustration can become deep seated leading to the development of a just-get-by culture focused on extrinsic gain. Believing that the company values creativity appears to act as a motivational force. Not only does it help fulfil stakeholders' intrinsic need to be creative, but it increases their willingness to work in areas less personally fulfilling for short periods of time.

Diversity is important as it enhances the cultural dynamic by adding variety and change, so helping to stimulate more energetic relationships. However, there is some disagreement about the extent to which diversity favours group cohesion and creative behaviour. Some argue (King and Anderson 1990; Sethi et al. 2002) that more homogeneous groups engender greater trust, so facilitating creativity. While others (Janis 1982) believe that homogeneous cultures encourage stagnation and group-think. It is important to consider what constitutes homogeneity and heterogeneity. Diversity of knowledge, experience and skills can bring valuable perspectives to a problem, helping people to think 'outside the box', but their presence does not necessarily lead to complete heterogeneity. We have suggested that creative cultures rely on choosing people whose core values are the same. They may come from a variety of backgrounds, and have differing views, but their fundamental values are aligned. When core values are the same, diversity of experience or skills does not have to lead to the disruptive heterogeneric cultures. Design Bridge provides a useful case in point. It employs a wide variety of people with different backgrounds and experiences. However, closer inspection reveals a common set of values that link people together and help generate a strong relational bond. The Design Bridge culture is homogeneous at its core but exhibits heterogeneous qualities in terms of skill, knowledge and experience mix. For creativity to occur cultures need to be both homogeneous and heterogeneous at different organisational and personal levels. Both need to occur for creative tension to exist.

Finally, a *desire to learn* needs to exist at both a personal and organisational level if a creative culture is to flourish. Continuous growth of knowledge is critical to the creative process as it enhances and improves inter-stakeholder understanding of behaviours, needs, desires, cultures and markets. Not only does this provide a breadth of perspective that can help in making novel connections, it also facilitates the development of trusting, cooperative relationships. In addition, providing learning opportunities and support reinforces the perception that managers are delivering on their promises, so strengthening relationships. Organisations should also consider the value of developing wider learning networks to include external stakeholders. This can be valuable, not only because it helps combine diverse knowledge, but also because it can facilitate increased understanding and trust between previously separate parties.

Achieving structural balance

We know that traditional bureaucratical models reduce trust and creativity and that rigid structures inhibit creativity by increasing fear of punishment and replacing risk taking with defensive egocentric behaviour. Such structures reduce information flows, impose rigid norms and controls on thinking, limit the ability to communicate and reduce intrinsic motivation. Also role specialisation and a focus on control reduce trust, information flow, open communication and the perception of support. There are too many organisations like this. According to Manville and Ober (2003): 'the entire shape of the modern company reflects a fundamental distrust of its members'. A thought that is also endorsed by Chan and Mauborgne (2003), who note that managers tend to assume that employees are always focused on self-interest and that it is therefore dangerous to give up power to them. Part of the reason for this tendency is the belief that others are motivated by the same things as ourselves. This is endorsed by research by Chip Heath of Stanford (Morse 2003) that shows that managers are not as good at understanding employee motivations as they think they are. Their assumption is that extrinsic rewards rather than intrinsic ones motivate employees. This in turn affects personal attitudes and motivation and impacts on the cooperative nature of stakeholder relationships.

Unfortunately, even organisations with so-called flat structures can exhibit hierarchical structures, supporting our view that most organisational design is just a variation of the bureaucratic model. This is not to say that flat structures inhibit creativity. There are many examples of how they can be valuable in building high-trust, creative organisations, as they enable faster decision making, ease of information flow and autonomy. However, success is reliant on the ability and willingness of senior management to forgo traditional power-play behaviour. Often, even when there is seeming autonomy, it is a parody, as real decision making remains centralised at board or senior managerial levels. The hierarchy still exists, although perhaps in a reduced and less formal configuration of roles and responsibilities.

The problem facing managers is that they have wider spans of control across a variety of subjects of which they often have little in-depth knowledge. The issue facing them again relates to trust: do they have sufficient belief in their subordinates and do they have sufficient self-belief to manage with limited knowledge? If not, then traditional forms of management and structures can reassert themselves, encouraging a more defensive, risk-averse political culture. It is important to recognise that today's workforce often enters industry with high levels of education and specialist training. As such, many can be viewed as educated, able and intrinsically motivated professionals, who work best in an environment that respects this intellectual ability. Structures that control or remove autonomy directly related to their sphere of interest will be met with hostility and suspicion.

The answer to the dilemma of structure may lie in the networks or communities proposed by Fukuyama (2001), Handy (2001) and Morgan (1997), where social capital, citizen behaviour and linked but autonomous networks are developed to facilitate constructive relationships. Members of creative organisations display citizen-type behaviour, wanting to do their best not only for themselves but for the team and the company. Design Bridge, IDEO, Gensler, Funcom and many of the other organisations researched illustrate this pattern by exhibiting openness, honesty and community-oriented behaviour that appears non-egocentric. The question is how to encourage citizen structures while maintaining operational efficiency. Goodwill alone is not enough. Highly creative people are often unable or unwilling to become involved with administrative or strategic business issues. A balanced framework that supports these activities, giving personal focus while helping to ensure strategic business objectives are met, is the answer.

The network 'spider plant' model put forward by Morgan (1997) is a structure that provides an interesting starting point, and is one that PAG echoes in its own organisational design. At the core of this model is the concept of a central supportive 'plant', from which autonomous plants can grow and operate while maintaining links with the central plant and other offshoots. In the case of PAG the first series of offshoots represent each brand: Aston Martin, Jaguar, Volvo, Lincoln and Land Rover. From these have grown more plants in the form of operational functions and geographical offices. In addition, around the whole network, a series of independent creativity and innovation centres revolve and interconnect with all the other offshoots. It may at first sound complicated, but if viewed in a spider plant context a simpler picture emerges of independent and self-organised groups that are able to call on a vast network of knowledge and resources to support and guide activities. There is a framework of control, vision and shared objectives, yet within these broad boundaries a large amount of autonomy exists.

This is similar to the idea of institutional transactive memory: a shared memory that helps people to know who has the knowledge to help solve a problem (see also Chapter 3 under Knowledge networks on '2 degrees of separation'). In his study of social epidemics, *The Tipping Point*, Malcolm Gladwell (2001) argues that this memory can only work in communities where size allows for cohesion. He calls this the Rule of 150. Communities of less than 150 people are likely to have personal knowledge of each other and to share a collective memory. Beyond 150 and organisations start communicating less well and personal relationships are diminished. The principle of 150 is espoused by Gore Associates, manufacturers of Gore-Tex, who never allow business units to grow larger than 150 people. They strip out formal management structures and as a result enjoy accelerated creativity:

> In a high-technology company like Gore, which relies for its market edge on its ability to innovate and react quickly to demanding and sophisticated customers, this kind of global memory system is critical. It makes the company incredibly efficient. It means that you move much faster to get things done or create teams of workers or find out an answer to a problem. It means that people in one part of the company can get access to the impressions and experience of people in a completely different part of the company.
>
> *(Gladwell 2001, p191)*

This focus on self-organisation is important in building trust, intrinsic motivation and relationships, while the supportive structure of the central plant provides a framework within which staff can function without fear. Such a framework should not be rigid. It is important that such networks are not allowed to develop into hierarchical structures that increase management levels and reduce autonomy. Within the agreed framework of support, each network can make strategic decisions and develop relationships with other offshoots or related stakeholders. If this is not allowed to occur, organisations run the risk of being perceived as untrustworthy and not delivering on their promises, reducing trust and the quality of relationships between senior managers and staff. It is important that this set of frameworks and structural boundaries should not be viewed in negative terms. We believe they can be seen as forces or pressures that develop creative tensions within the work environment while giving focus and support. Boundaries can help organisations to focus and function; people need to understand fundamental roles, rules, objectives and processes, however flexible or fluid, if they are to deliver value. The key is to identify where the balance lies for each organisation or network and to ensure that they do not remain static but are open to change through negotiation or organic development. If frameworks or networks become rigid or too constraining, hierarchies may form, reducing self-organisation and citizen-behaviour-based relationships and interstakeholder trust, so inhibiting the creative process.

A final question: does physical separation hinder creativity? The majority of current thinking exalts the need to knock down walls and bring everyone into the same space. Without doubt this can improve information flow and help reduce the perception of hierarchies, even if they still exist. However, our research suggests that its influence may not be as considerable as some people believe. Certainly physical barriers can reduce ease of face-to-face communication and the potential for chance meeting which is important to the creative process. However, if the culture is open and trusting, physical separation may not matter as much. A number of companies we have worked with over the years exist in warren-like layouts yet consistently deliver creativity. What they have all have in common are strong positive cultures of understanding and belief in a clear set of shared values. We are not saying breaking down physical barriers is not valuable, just that it is not the be all and end all that so many managers think it is.

Conclusion

It is important that organisations seek to develop creative communities that exhibit cultural and structural balance between personal creative needs and the demands of a commercially oriented organisation. It is essential that managers are clear on what their brand values are and develop the right balance of people, structures and systems to facilitate creativity within this context. It is important that they do not apply rigid management models and ignore the personal aspect of the creative process. Assuming what has worked before, or what works elsewhere, will work within the present environment is dangerous. It can signal limited emotional intelligence and lead to inappropriate strategy development. We believe that it is vital for managers to understand stakeholder needs, expectations and desires and not treat them as stereotypical homogeneous groups.

When considering how to develop a creative culture we conclude that senior managers need to start by ensuring recruitment processes do not focus solely on functional ability, but also on breadth of skills, underpinned by similar core personal values and characteristics in line with the brand. The objective is to create a diverse, yet similarly grounded, culture, balancing homogeneity and heterogeneity. We also believe that trust is an underpinning construct without which creative relationships and cultures cannot develop. Without trust it is unlikely that stakeholders will openly and honestly communicate, take risks, be motivated and cooperate. Without trust a culture of enjoyment will not develop, even though the personal needs of staff dictate its presence as an intrinsic motivator and facilitator to creative idea generation.

If trust is not at the core of the corporate brand, diversity, in terms of work practices, knowledge and experience will be harder to encourage and develop. This will lead to a reduction in the breadth of organisational knowledge, prevent the inclusion of unusual stimuli, ideas and perspectives, so reducing the quality of relationships and debate through group-think or hostility. However, this book also argues that organisations should maintain a core of homogeneity, in terms of basic personal and business values, among employees based on the brand. Without this, confusion, conflict or chaos will result. Finally, it is suggested that creative brands exhibit a desire and commitment to learning that help them build trust with internal and external stakeholders. This encourages commitment and creative behaviour and helps facilitate closer communication and understanding with audiences. In addition, it helps develop a culture that has a wide breadth and depth of knowledge, so enhancing creative debate through greater understanding of contexts and possibilities.

With reference to structure, it is clear that traditional rigid hierarchies reduce trust, preventing open communication, learning, risk taking, cooperation, diversity and motivation. Such structures create a non-trusting ethic, based on control and power relationships within which egocentric behaviour can flourish. However, this book proposes creative organisations do need some structures and systems to help them manage complex information and projects within both a business and creative context. The answer lies in creating structural balance between the individual needs of staff and commercial requirements. Where balance is achieved, trusting relationships are developed through the delivery of autonomy, learning and support, within a framework that provides the resources and administrative support necessary for the brand to grow and deliver value.

Finally, network and self-organisational models provide the strongest structural foundation for future company design. By providing a framework of resources and knowledge networks that support staff, a brand can balance business needs with creative freedom. Such structures encourage autonomy and help facilitate the trust-based relationships, citizen behaviour and social capital that we believe are fundamental to the creative processes.

LESSONS FOR CREATIVITY

- Creativity requires a balance to be met between personal and commercial needs

- Managers have to shift their focus away from controlling staff and start understanding their needs, perceptions and relationships

- Clear understanding of your brand values provides the foundation from which creative structures can be developed and systems managed

- Trust lies at the heart of creativity. Managers must deliver on their promises and nurture trusting relationships between stakeholders

- Creative organisations maintain a core of staff homogeneity in terms of basic personal and business values yet encourage diversity of skills and knowledge

- Creativity requires structure as well as freedom if chaos is to be prevented and energy focused

- Network structures provide the balance between support and autonomy

Notes

1   The historian of ideas, Michel Foucault, when interviewed about the nature of liberty and its relationship to architecture, observed that people often thought about architecture in terms of its ability to liberate (or oppress) people. However, he also stated that creating buildings could not be functionally liberating, because liberty is a practice; liberty is what must be exercised. We can make the same judgement about creativity. Creativity is not a thing, it is a practice.

2   The innovation consultancy, IDEO are keen proselytisers of this idea of cross-pollination and call it the 'alchemy of innovation'.

3   Sternberg, R.J., Kaufman, J.C. and Pretz, J.E. argue in *The Creativity Conundrum* (2002, Psychology Press, New York) that creativity is about things that are novel, high in quality and appropriate. They also put forward the view that creative contributions can be defined in eight different ways.

4   While Nordstrom employees go out of their way to deliver outstanding service – even personally delivering items to customers' homes – they are also highly accountable in performance terms.

5   In Jim Collins' book *Good to Great* (2001 Random House Business Books, London), the great companies averaged cumulative stock returns 6.9 times the general market in the 15 years following their transition points.

3 Designing Creativity

From Gaudi's organic, fantasy-driven, Sagrada Familia cathedral in Barcelona to Philippe Starck's chic, playful and surreal Sanderson hotel in London's West End, design and architecture have constantly provided examples of inspired, visionary and transformational creativity. However, they have also provided the world with creative turkeys of such magnitude that we often gasp at their apparent ineptitude or lack of insight into the needs of clients, end users or society. As many a designer or architect will tell you 'Doctors bury their mistakes but we have to live with ours'. Unfortunately, people have a tendency to remember and even revel in failure rather than focusing on the multitude of benefits these disciplines have brought us. This problem, combined with numerous celebrity designers and the occasional prima donna, has generated a negatively embedded perception of design agencies and architectural practices. To many they are unprofessional, expensive and mysterious organisations that may occasionally produce something of value but often develop ideas that have no bearing or benefit in the real world, that overrun budgets and that never finish on time.

This is an unfair and dangerous view for businesses to have. Design generates competitive advantage, it can reinforce positive brand attributes, provide tangible functional benefits and incite excitement and passion. Design continually questions the status quo, reinvents, and refreshes and revitalises our businesses and world. It is at the heart of new product development and new brand development; it provides solutions and generates new opportunities. Without design, businesses would remain static, devoid of new products and services, brands would become homogenous and bland and life, dull, boring and difficult. The design process is by definition a creative process: risk taking will and should occur. The key for organisations is learning how to focus and manage their creative energy, limit the potential for catastrophic failure and increase the potential for trans-formational change.

The key to success does not lie solely with effective project management systems nor with slavish adherence to the plethora of management models taught on today's MBA courses. The companies we look at in this chapter are all responsible for numerous award-winning, commercially successful designs. They are able to balance creativity with business savvy and, although they vary in size, func-tion and geographical location, they all recognise that it is their cultural foundation that gives them the ability to be creatively successful. Design Bridge, a UK-based but international design agency with offices in Amsterdam and Singapore, specialises in pack-aging design and corporate identity for a number of blue-chip clients including Unilever and Nestlé. Although comparatively small compared to the other companies in this book it still employs around 150 full-time staff and has a turnover in excess of £10 million. IDEO, the Californian-based product design firm and innovation company is globally renowned for its creative solutions, such as the first mouse for the Apple Macintosh, the Palm V PDA and Prada's Manhattan flagship store. With eight offices around the world it develops about 90 new products every year. The architectural and design practice Gensler is the final organisation discussed in this chapter. Like IDEO it has a significant global presence, employing 1600 people across 24 offices with a turnover of $305 million in 2002.

People power

Culture is about people; it is formed from the perceptions, expecta-tions and interactions of people within a context of structures and systems. It develops from, and reacts to, work and cultural practices that in turn inform the norms and values that are the foundation on which cultural behaviour and personal dispositions are formed. Understanding and managing cultural personality is a key require-ment for any organisation wishing to increase creative output due to the personal and relationship-driven nature of the creative process. As Tim Brown, IDEO's president and CEO, notes:

> If you believe that creativity and innovation are a team effort; if you take the view that there are a lot of things to do with creativity and innovation that are risky, then you need to establish a culture that supports all that. We would argue that culture is the foundation from which you build everything else. So if your culture forces your people to behave in non-collaborative ways or exposes people to the risks they're taking in negative ways, then you won't get innovation; you won't get sustained innovation. We're in the business of routine innovation. We need to be able to do this day in day out. It has to be continu-ously supported. It has to be in the DNA of the place. We believe it's the culture that provides that.
>
> *(Interview with author dated 21 August 2003)*

For IDEO this means understanding that culture is an organic being that cannot and should not be managed in a traditional control-oriented manner. Instead it requires managers to be mindful and insightful of their and other stakeholders' actions with relation to the norms and values that lie at the heart of the company. They believe that this translates into valuing people, placing them at the heart of the company and ensuring that managers are involved with and aware of their needs. This view is echoed by CEO Ed Friedrichs (Gensler) and Chief Executive Branding and Packaging, Jill Marshall (Design Bridge) both of whom strongly believe in forming long-term relationships with staff based on understanding needs and delivering tailored solutions to each member of staff. Marshall believes that such a process of active and continuous engagement with staff is key to developing and maintaining a close 'family' culture that balances freedom of expression with commercial responsibility. For Design Bridge this freedom is expressed in many ways; casual and person-alised dress styles, flexible working hours, personal down time, freedom to visit exhibitions or other centres of stimuli, personalised work practices and, most importantly, the ability to manage and direct projects from within the team. Similarly IDEO and Gensler encourage and resource such freedom, believing that it motivates staff, adds to the organisational knowledge bank and promotes diverse and critical debate.

Brown, Friedrichs and Marshall all agree that such a people-focused approach provides a foundation from which a trust-based culture can develop. However they recognise that no amount of nurturing will work if the right type of people are not in place. People are key. Each company spends a great deal of time, money and effort searching for and developing staff. They want people who will add to the mix, challenge the status quo and bring passion to their work. They want people who want to make a difference, who want to engage with other people and ideas and who will live the brand with honesty and energy. For them personality is as valuable as craft skill or experience, because they recognise that creativity is based on positive trust-based relationships. What is interesting is that none of the companies follows the rigid, structured interviewing processes favoured by many of today's businesses. Instead they follow a far more collaborative, flexible, equitable and intuitive process that not only ensures skills and core competencies are matched but also helps maintain the optimum balance of personality mix. Interviews take the form of informal meetings, discussions and socially based gatherings where candidates become immersed in the organisation's culture for significant periods of time. More often than not each company has already developed a relationship with, or has knowledge of, the candidate through freelance work, previous experience, or personal recommendation, thus giving them greater insight into the person. Marshall explains:

> Design is all about relationships; you have to be able to get on with the people you work with and work for if you want to do something special. When I interview people I'm looking for skill and interesting experience but in the end it comes down to the person. I carry out my desert island test. If I was stranded on an island with this person could I survive with them or would I want to kill them after the first week?
>
> *(Interview with author dated 25 September 2001)*

Although this view and process may seem arbitrary and unprofessional it actually requires a great deal of emotional intelligence as well as a deep understanding of the organisational brand. Not only does it require directors to have a grasp of the skill needs within the company, they also need to understand the personality, culture and needs of the brand as well as each team or department if they are to successfully match people to positions. At IDEO, Gensler and Design Bridge the proof of the pudding is in the eating. Not only are these companies leaders in their field, constantly producing award-winning, commercially successful designs, they have extremely low staff turnover, a rarity in such a volatile industry. People come to the companies and stay, not for 2 or 3 years but for ten, fifteen or twenty years, sometimes for the majority of their working life. They marry within the company, some may leave to have babies or raise families, but many return. This is exactly what the companies want. It makes them competitively powerful because their staff are committed, understand the brand and customers instinctively and are willing to engage collaboratively. Consider the point Friedrichs makes about Gensler:

> So the culture is very much driven around making a career with the firm. All of our benefits programmes, our education programmes, the relationship we want people to have at all levels of the firm … it needs to be a very rich participatory environment. We have a much more collaborative, collegial, team-based method of working where people can be reasonably sure that they can see a project through from conception to implementation. So culturally, everything in the firm is structured to be that way. And so we have better longevity than other firms, certainly better continuity of personnel that has led to better long-term relationships with clients. That's deeply embedded in the culture. Even to the point that we keep in touch with people after they leave. We want them to come back because we know they're excellent people. We have a boomerang programme.
>
> *(Interview with author dated 21 August 2003)*

Knowledge networks

Another characteristic that our companies share is the existence of large and diverse knowledge networks that continuously feed each organisation. There is a joint understanding that creativity cannot occur in either a social or knowledge vacuum, nor should companies rely on a narrow band of specialised knowledge in their quest for creativity. IDEO and Gensler hold dominant positions in the vanguard of this thinking, both implementing wide-ranging strategies to enhance the breadth and depth of their knowledge.

IDEO recognises that to be continually creative you must be continually stimulated. It understands that traditional management methods restrict the quality, variety and flow of information around a company, so limiting the stimulus available to staff. It also realises that overreliance on market research can lead to mediocrity and stagnation. Instead it has developed a knowledge-brokering network that focuses on sharing information across stakeholder boundaries and is based on the belief that breadth of knowledge is equally as important as depth. For IDEO, creativity starts with insight. This not only means direct insight into the specific problem area but also a much wider range of insight into related and potentially related contexts. Keeping knowledge in its functionally based silo is not seen as an option to IDEO, as such siloisation is the enemy of creativity. Brown argues that to be creative you have to have new and different understandings and perspectives and the more perspectives you have the better equipped you are to look at the world anew and to generate original solutions. For him this creative fuel comes from people – diverse, knowledgeable, communicative and passionate people – who bring energy, ideas and breadth to debate:

> You have to have as many ways of providing that fuel as you can. So you need creative people with different perspectives. The people who fit within IDEO are not the narrow, single-discipline experts. You do have to have depth, but also breadth. The breadth is all about empathy for other perspectives and points of view, to the extent that people know how to work in those other disciplines – so designers know how to be human factors people, or designers know how to be engineers. Our best people are the ones that can do that. They get to look at the world from a number of different perspectives.
>
> *(Interview with author dated 21 August 2003)*

It is IDEO's ability to look at the world from different viewpoints, to understand, to feel, to envisage possibilities, that sets it apart.[1] Again it is IDEO's culture that forms the foundation of this world. In Brown's words it is their stakeholders' openness, inquisitiveness and lack of scepticism that provide the fuel for creative stimulation. Not only does this facilitate creative debate, it encourages teams and clients to approach the design process in new and more interactive ways. It involves clients, end users and wider audiences in workshops, input sessions and role-play scenarios in an attempt to inspire and gain greater insight into issues. Its process is not about market validation, it is about gaining new insights through co-creation. It stays away from traditional market research methods such as focus groups and favours unfocused groups. In these situations a very diverse group of people who have some interest or connection with the issue are brought together and work with the design team and generate ideas. For example, a group recently working on a shoe project included an SM (sadomasochism) fanatic. Her input was seen as vital because it introduced a totally new way of looking at and understanding shoes. Traditional research methods would never be able to provide such a perspective yet companies still insist on employing them. It is the richness and diversity of knowledge combined with IDEO's culture of openness that allows it to develop and utilise new and exciting insights, unhindered by traditional and limited processes.

Similarly Design Bridge and Gensler recognise the importance of widening their sources of stimulation and knowledge. Like IDEO they value new perspectives, however they also understand that as their industry becomes more complex they cannot be expected to know everything. They realise that broad knowledge networks increase their intellectual capital, enabling them to draw on expert opinions as and when they need, so providing clients with the definitive knowledge they demand. Design Bridge strongly advocates developing joint client–agency networks through formal workshops and conferences as well as more informal, socially based strategies. It feels this not only adds to its ability to see problems from a number of perspectives but it also helps to develop a trusting relationship with the client. For Gensler this view has become an embedded strategy based on the idea of '2 degrees of separation'. As Friedrichs recalls, the strategy started 15 years ago when he realised the value of leveraging stakeholder connections:

> So back 15 years ago we started thinking about how we could deliver state-of-the-art thinking to our clients. And you had to start thinking about how to use

the networks that existed in the firm. So we started this campaign that you needed a maximum of 2 degrees of separation. This meant that you had to know someone who knew who the definitive expert was; you needed to know who knew stuff about stuff. It's about a world of connections. You could probably find someone whose personal passion was carbon fibre technology; they would meet up with the definitive expert – that's 2 degrees of separation. So we started this campaign internally about 2 degrees of separation.

(Interview with author dated 21 August 2003)

He sees this strategy as valuable not only to him and his clients but to all the members of the network because the nature of the relationship is equitable. Each network member has something special to offer, so collectively they form a deep and rich knowledge bank, which any member can access. It is not a formal network but a virtual family that is continuously growing and developing, stimulating and debating. For Gensler, like IDEO, this network allows it to approach projects from a multitude of viewpoints that helps it redefine contexts and needs. As a result it may view an airport as echoing a shopping mall, an office echoing a hotel. Changing the nature of the context and working with the relevant experts has helped Gensler radically redesign many spaces.

This strategy was employed in 1998 when Gensler was commissioned to redesign the Sherman Oaks Galleria in Southern California. This 3-level, covered mall, once a pop culture phenomenon, had gone into decline and had been empty for four years when Gensler was invited in by the developer to brainstorm some possible solutions. Using its diverse internal and external networks it was able to put together a team that began asking fundamental questions about the context of a shopping mall and its role in the community such as: What were people looking for? What was missing? What would they gravitate towards? What were the competing places? By including people from the planning, retail, hospitality, education and office sectors they were able to develop a new vision for the centre. Instead of simply revamping the existing mall they changed its very nature into a lifestyle centre. They split the centre in half; one half was used as office space while the other was transformed from a closed mall into a covered, natural-air environment housing restaurants, theatres, a health club and spa as well as retail units.

External collaboration

Creative cultures focus not only on understanding and meeting the needs of internal stakeholders, but are also strongly outward-looking. Focusing on the client is an embedded brand value among our three companies. However, it goes much further than traditional sales orientation: they are passionate about engaging with and building long-term collaborative partnerships with all external stake-holders. Unlike some 'creative' companies they are not egocentric prima donnas who reject outside input. Instead they relish engage-ment with external stakeholders because they realise that cultures cannot become creative if they remain locked in ivory towers. IDEO attempts to involve clients at all stages of a project, making the process as transparent as possible believing that:

> If you do it in a complete enough way, expectation management becomes a self-managing thing. The more black box you make the process the more you have to worry about expectation management. There's no visibility – they (clients) can't prepare themselves and they can't prepare you. So that's why we've tried to move towards being more transparent and more open – there's more participation, involvement and buy-in.
>
> *(Interview with author dated 21 August 2003)*

The value of this process was made clear when IDEO was commissioned to develop a surgical tool for sinusitis operations. The collaborative approach it used relied heavily on involving the client, Gyrus ENT, and a team of expert surgeons inputting ideas, co-creating concepts and co-developing and testing prototypes. As Brown realised, not only was this concurrent process highly cost effective, but, by reducing the need for significant redesign, it also created a strong sense of ownership among the external team. This provided IDEO with a number of well-placed, influential champions within the client company who were determined to sell the idea up through the organisation and it also ensured the existence of passionate, expert and independent fans willing to endorse the product.

Another design organisation that embraces a co-creation culture is Marketplace Design. This retail branding agency, based near Oxford in the UK, is relatively small by IDEO and Gensler standards and yet has produced significant work for clients such as Audi,

Porsche, Lexus, the Post Office and Cadbury by actively engaging with as many stakeholders as possible. A good example of this was a project for Fairline, a global luxury-yacht manufacturer. Marketplace was asked to design and develop a globally effective retail environment that would pull the Fairline brand together and deliver consistent messages and experiences to customers. Immediately the agency began the co-creation process by working with the client to interpret and develop a brief that would provide meaningful focus yet would be flexible enough to allow adaptation as broader stakeholder engagement occurred. Once the essential parameters were established, the company and client began a three-month programme of external stakeholder discussion, input and investigation. Unlike many research programmes it was not confined to quantitatively based questionnaires but relied on much broader and deeper discussions, workshops and involvement with the brand. The objective was to gain an instinctive understanding of the brand, its values, personality, desires and relationship with customers and dealers as well as the expectations and needs of key audiences.

Such a process was not cheap and involved significant travel for both design team and client, as well as the occasional boat trip. However, it was seen as central to the process, as it not only increased the understanding of the brand and its audience, but also helped to develop a strong bond between the team, client and dealers, with each actively engaging and contributing to idea generation and development. This resulted in a high degree of project ownership and trust, particularly between design team and client, which Managing Director Bryan Brown felt facilitated higher levels of creativity:

> It was really great to get in there with the client and their dealers. We were able to spend time getting to know them, what they wanted, what the problems were and how they felt about the brand. The client was really up for it anyway, but working with him so closely really helped us get into his head and get to know him. We were able to involve him in our thinking, show him we understood what was going on and where the brand could go. He really got into it, which was great because it stopped being them and us and became organic ... involving the dealers was especially important because they were going to have to fund individual developments and they were a bit sceptical at first. As we

spent more time with them we were able to win them over and show them the potential of what could be.

(Interview with author dated 7 February 2002)

This co-creative process required large amounts of front-end investment but proved cost-effective as well as creatively successful. Early concepts were well received by the client's board, dealers and customers, with development and successful implementation occurring swiftly after. This belief and passion in external collaboration is a core construct of any creative brand as it forms a set of values that focus on equitable engagement, cooperation and understanding of a wide range of needs and expectations that in turn inform group behaviour and disposition.

Conclusion

The agencies in this chapter illustrate how clear, positive cultures provide focus and momentum to the creative process. In particular they highlight the value strong cultural understanding can bring to environments by providing an embedded vision that directs disposition and action. Managers at Design Bridge, Gensler and IDEO all exhibit high levels of emotional intelligence in the way they encourage the development and maintenance of personal relationships, collaboration and openness. They value people and they value diversity and this underpins their attitudes towards people, relationships and doing business. For them creativity is about insight, making abstract connections and seeing things in new ways. They realise that limited breadth and depth of knowledge will hinder their envisioning ability and have set about developing networks of knowledge that they are able to tap into to draw upon diverse views and experience. Not only does this enhance the intellectual capital of the companies, it also helps them redefine problems and add significant value to their work. Above all they understand that equitable collaboration is at the heart of the creative process.

LESSONS FOR CREATIVITY

- Creative cultures are truly representative of their staff and should develop accordingly

- Personality fit is as important as skill mix. 'Liking' is a key component of a creative culture as it increases emotive bonds and helps develop trust

- Creative cultures exhibit high levels of inquisitiveness as well as rich depth and breadth of knowledge

- Diverse internal and external knowledge networks increase an organisation's ability to think creatively

- Traditional sources of knowledge and research can limit creativity if solely relied on as they limit the diversity of perspectives brought to bear on a problem

- Collaborative relationships are at the heart of the creative process

- Engaging with all stakeholders increases the depth and breadth of knowledge and increases the level of trust between parties

Note

1   IDEO have recently released a set of cards at $49 that illustrate one methodology they use to stimulate out-of-the-box thinking. Each pack contains a series of 'suits' that provide users with different scenarios, hints and methodological approaches. Not only does this help people view problems from different perspectives but it also encourages them to empathise fully with end users.

4 Managing for Creativity

Introduction

The Nobel Prize winning chemist Linus Pauling once said that to get good ideas, 'you have a lot of ideas and throw away the bad ones' (Csikszentmihalyi 1997, p116). More profoundly, the much quoted Pogo the Possum, said in Walt Kelly's cartoon strip, 'we are surrounded by insurmountable opportunity' (cited in Cringely 1996, p297). These two quotations sum up the managerial challenge on creativity, which will be tackled in this chapter and illustrated in the next by the examples of film company Aardman Animations and games company Funcom. Pauling's aphorism indicates that organisations should generate as many ideas as possible on the principle that there will be a gem or two among them. While a highly creative individual can, by himself, be a significant source of ideas, if the creativity of others is not captured the size of the pool of ideas will be reduced and full use will not be made of the intellectual capital of the organisation. Of course, the problem with success is managing the results – which brings us to Pogo. If the organisation does become good at generating ideas, it then has the problem of evaluating and implementing. Some ideas will be better than others, but to maintain commitment among employees every idea needs to be reviewed, feedback provided and ideas that progress need to be implemented with sensitivity. In this chapter we propose that this requires managers to focus on developing and maintaining trust-based employee relationships in order to facilitate and maintain creative behaviour. Without such relationships, cooperation, commitment and creative idea generation and implementation will be prevented because of fear, mistrust, frustration and lack of intrinsic motivation.

Leadership not dictatorship

George Orwell (1981, p100) in an essay on Charles Dickens wrote, 'you can only create if you can care'. He goes on to point out that the strength of Dickens – 'the final secret of his inventiveness' – lies in his strong beliefs. Caring is also a prerequisite of organisational creativity. Managers and employees will only contribute their ideas if (a) they believe in the organisation's purpose and ideology (and/or a project's purpose) and (b) they feel that they and their contributions will be valued and supported by the organisation. If people do not experience (a) they will not commit and effectively contribute and if they do not experience (b) they will become fearful or frustrated and begin to lose personal respect for senior management. This in turn reduces staff motivation and commitment, encourages passivity and limits the development of strong creative relationships. Eventually if employees believe their efforts will not be appreciated or valued they will stop trying to come up with new ideas. Managers cannot simply command employees to be creative. Rather they need to manage the culture, understand the motivations of employees, inspire them to fulfil their creative potential, set significant problems that stretch and develop employees' abilities through a process of challenge and response and provide good feedback. Their role is both champion and mentor, providing autonomy within specified boundaries that focus creative energy.

Being a creativity champion

Much of the literature on creativity stresses the heroic, creative individual. Undoubtedly, these people are both inspirational and exciting and often they strongly influence the organisational culture. Yet the inspiration of one individual cannot be effective without like-minded supporters. Our research suggests that, once organisations acquire any sense of scale, the primary role of the creative individual changes from creator to champion. This means less doing and more guiding. Also, as many organisations are resistant to new ideas, a creative individual needs allies. If this is to be realised there should be several creativity champions who are open to new and challenging ideas. Rather than a lone individual fighting against an indifferent system, this champions' network helps to foster a culture where creativity is supported. An environment develops where creativity is integrated into the organisational fabric and a balance is achieved between business efficiency and creativity. When creativity gets divorced from commercial reality, as were the innovations of Xerox PARC,[1] good ideas are missed.

To help ensure the connection with business performance requires creativity champions to have a strong identification with the organisational ideology and to understand the frameworks or boundaries of creativity. This is helped when the champions of creativity represent more business-oriented departments as well as the obvious homes of creativity, such as the research or design department. The CEO of British Airways Rod Eddington is seen by his staff as such a leader. During the extremely difficult trading conditions since September 11 British Airways has faced serious operational, financial and competitive difficulties. However, staff are both optimistic and energised about the future, seeing the charismatic and creative leadership of Rod Eddington as the driving force. As Peter Lynam director of operations, maintenance and planning observes:

> If you look right at the top, the whole atmosphere over the last few years has changed dramatically. If you ask people have things improved by having an Australian in charge, they will say yes. Not only is he extraordinarily knowledgeable about the industry, which attracts respect, he's an Aussie, so he has that sense of humour and a way about him. He is not easy to work for all the time mind, but he really provides momentum, vision and energy. The atmosphere is terrific, it's an unbelievable change in 3 or 4 years.
>
> *(Interview with author dated 11 July 2003)*

As this quote helps to illustrate, 'creativity champion' is not a title on a business card, but rather a descriptor of attitude. It requires people who have passion and a belief in the importance of finding new and better ways of doing things. These are people who care and are capable of encouraging others to care.

Managers as mentors

Creative champions believe in the value of creativity and actively promote the development of creative cultures. However, such beliefs must be communicated to others and support provided if creative strategies are to be successfully implemented. This is the manager as mentor – the power of which is demonstrated in all the companies we have included in this book. This ability to mentor requires managers to possess emotional intelligence, which can be defined as someone's ability to be self-aware, self-regulating, self-motivating, empathetic and socially skilled (Goleman 2001). This area of study has become mainstream in business since the publication of Daniel Goleman's book *Emotional Intelligence* (1995). Goleman and others (Mayer and Salovey 1997, Bar-On 2000) argue that a person's emotional intelligence and cognitive intelligence are interwoven rather than independent. In a business context this is important, because if an organisation assesses individuals solely on their cognitive intelligence, it will ignore attributes that are important to effective leadership. When it comes to overseeing creative processes the ability to recognise emotions in oneself and in others and to manage those emotions so that growth and learning are stimulated is vital. The implication of this is that managers of creative teams should have the emotional intelligence to manage people of often diverse backgrounds to make the most of their collective knowledge. This suggests an ideal of managers who have good emotional intelligence. However, it is also possible for social and emotional competencies to be developed with 'sustained effort and a systematic program' (Emmerling and Goleman 2003). From our work it is clear that employees want managers to lend support and provide learning and inspiration, while allowing employees the freedom to experiment and challenge established norms. They need someone to whom they can turn when problems arise, support is needed or another view required. In addition, they need to believe that help and support will be forthcoming even if they do not specifically require it at that time.

Mentoring can not only help give focus and spread knowledge, it can also generate the sense of safety needed to encourage risk taking. The normal expectation becomes one of controlled risk. We believe that it is vital for managers to believe in the value of mentoring as a creative facilitation model that requires them to understand how to balance support and freedom within their environments. There is broad agreement that the capacity to support and nurture is a fundamental leadership characteristic. Leadership requires characteristics such as self-awareness, empathy, trustworthy behaviour and social skills if meaningful relationships are to be developed. Only when employees believe that their managers are trustworthy will goodwill and commitment emerge. Once this belief exists, employees are more likely to take risks and act in a creative manner, believing that managers will seek to support them and protect them from difficulties or unpredicted change.

Mentoring requires the ability to balance autonomy with support. It is crucial that managers look at each member of staff on an individual basis, and tailor the mentoring style adopted accordingly. To assume that all employees have similar coping skills and strategies can be dangerous. If management is seen to lack supportive or mentoring traits, by appearing laissez-faire or risk-averse, employees start to think they can have no real control or input into projects and that creative ideas may not be supported if considered to be too original or risky. A lack of supportive trust-based leadership reduces levels of trust, respect and motivation. The resulting climate will not be conducive to creative behaviour. Cultures can become aggressive, dysfunctional or creatively passive with employees feeling neglected, frustrated or fearful. Equally, too much support may be perceived as overcontrolling and may lead to political, risk-averse or conflict-oriented relationships.

Controlled chaos

Communicate support and deliver your promises

In a knowledge economy employees are typically highly educated, intrinsically motivated and potentially volatile people. Although such people can be stubborn and egocentric, they are also highly sensitive to environmental nuances and are affected by perceptions of support and trust within their relationship networks. If they believe that promises have not, or will not, be kept, or that support will be withheld, they can become demotivated, uncooperative and unlikely to engage in creative behaviour with stakeholders. Managers who develop strategies that communicate and illustrate benevolent attitudes to experimentation, risk taking and other forms of creative behaviour are most likely to promote creativity.

The importance of motivation in the creative process is a subject that has recently received some significant attention. In particular, the importance of intrinsic motivators, such as achievement, recognition, the work itself, responsibility, growth and advancement, has been demonstrated by Teresa Amabile and her colleagues (Amabile and Conti 1994 and Amabile et al. 1996). To date, most research and management practice has focused on either extrinsic motivators, such as supervision, company policy, working conditions, salary, status and security, or intrinsically oriented reward schemes.[2] Although some extrinsic rewards are important in providing a perception of value, they do not facilitate creativity unless balanced against intrinsic motivators. We believe this framing of the problem to some extent misses the point. Intrinsic motivators, do not alone provide the motivational foundations for creativity. It is important for managers to realise that an individual's level of intrinsic motivation is not a fixed quantity. It is a variable influenced by the person's assessment of management's ability to deliver on promises and expectations. This assessment conditions working relationships and a person's desire and willingness to engage creatively.

Our research has revealed that the level of intrinsic motivation is significantly influenced by the degree of trust present between stakeholders. The issue of how trust is developed and managed is complex, but is based on clear, honest communication and action from all sides. Chapter 2 illustrated the importance of recruitment procedures in developing cultural fit and providing an informal contract between company and professional. Explicit and implicit promises are made or perceived by both parties and expectations developed. For creative people these expectations may include perceptions of project type, creative potential, degree of autonomy, resource allocation, levels of personal challenge, career enhancement and potential for enjoyment. All are key motivation determinants and any perception that they have not been delivered, or made available, can reduce trust and lead to a reduction in motivation. In addition, if employees do not deliver on their promises, or meet the expectations of management, the organisation may re-evaluate its level of trust and take punitive action, thereby affecting motivational balance.

As the relationship continues, and the staff member becomes part of the organisational network, it is vital that support is offered and given. The companies in this book highlight the positive impact of senior management and interteam support, with staff not only feeling secure and able to experiment but also expressing benign feelings towards individual managers and the organisation. They believe that other team members respect their intelligence and abilities and that their ideas would be supported and developed through positive debate. In short they feel that the organisation is on their side and will help them generate the most creative solutions possible within the constraints of the project.

Deliver autonomy and ownership

Knowledge economy employees seem not to respond well to autocratic styles of management. Rather they require their professional status, personal needs and individualism to be recognised and supported. Managers who operate a policy of self-organisation increase the potential for project and team choice and grant staff a sense of project ownership. One of the problems facing managers is how to achieve this and maintain balance between individual and commercial needs. A sense of autonomy is particularly important for highly creative people who are rarely interested in administrative or business roles.

This helps underline a vital question: how can managers deliver self-regulation to creative individuals, such as designers, who often subordinate business imperatives? Much of the literature relating to self-organisation and creative organisations as networks (Handy 2001, Henry 2001a, 2001b, Fukuyama 2001 and Morgan 1997) does not deal in detail with this issue. To assume that blanket autonomy is the answer is wrong. The creative process is personal, and individualistic. We suggest that the answer lies in providing a framework within which people can work with freedom to express their individuality and experiment within a commercial context. In doing so we emphasise the need to develop a holistic framework that focuses on supporting staff rather than simply ensuring that operational targets are met. Aardman Animations and Funcom are able to create such environments due to managers' level of understanding of employees' personal needs and styles. In these organisations, and others in this book, managers do not seek to control employees but rather to provide them with support and direction, respecting their creative talents yet understanding their limitations. The majority of employees understand and appreciate this form of informal contract, not seeing it as a controlling mechanism but rather something that frees up their time and creative energy. Similarly PAG, British Airways, IDEO and Design Bridge all provide clear boundaries, role responsibilities and clarity of direction through active communication and engagement with staff. To some degree, such frameworks appear to reduce both the frustrations and feelings of fear or uncertainty held by individuals when dealing with areas outside their competence. The framework provides security and focus, granting freedom to experiment and for self-expression in a supportive environment. This is particularly valuable for employees who interact with customers on a regular basis – the framework sets a boundary within which people are free to give tailored and effective service.

Although many organisations disappoint in their service delivery, companies such as Nordstrom, Virgin Atlantic and the IceHotel in the Arctic Circle excel, because they respect employees. Kerstin Nilsson, one of the founders of the IceHotel says about employees:

> I think attitude is the most important. We meet everyone who wants to work here. We interview them personally and we explain to them about the hotel and how it is to work in such a cold climate. We listen to them very carefully: what their opinion is about taking care of people; how they would solve different problems. We also tell them very clearly what expectations we have.
>
> *(Interview with author dated 27 March 2003)*

As this quotation suggests, commitment comes from enabling employees not only to shape projects but also to help determine the development of the organisation. The philosopher, Peter Koestenbaum (Koestenbaum and Block 2001, p290), says, 'our institutions are transformed the moment we decide they are ours to create'.

Employees welcome the opportunity to choose projects, as this communicates trust and benevolent behaviour on the part of management. As a result intrinsic motivation is stimulated. Granting people a degree of autonomy in their work bolsters creativity and the status of people within the organisation. For intrinsic motivation to swell, trust needs to exist between stakeholders and this requires finesse on the part of the management, which needs to balance the prospect of innovation against the need for control.

It is worth remembering here the symbolic role of management, as even seemingly insignificant restrictions on employees can signal a poor understanding of needs and expectations. Anything perceived to reduce individual freedom or that communicates poor understanding of the professional status of staff, can impact negatively on levels of trust and creative behaviour. Creative people exhibit high degrees of individual behaviour, often viewing themselves as non-conformists, fashionable and challenging. Sometimes it is important to encourage this percep-tion by, for example, flexibility over working hours or time off – at Quiksilver, management recognises that employees' passion for surfing is an asset and that when the swells are good they should be encour-aged to take advantage of them, whether it is during working time or not. At Design Bridge, IDEO and PAG designers and staff are encour-aged to take personal time out to visit exhibitions, galleries and confer-ences or to try out new products, services or experiences that they feel might be interesting or valuable to their work. For these companies and many of the others we have highlighted, this seeming relaxedness does not lead to indiscipline because people know they have to be responsible and they are expected to perform and deliver on time.

Overall, the greater the sense of project ownership people feel, the greater the commitment and the stronger the personal connec-tion. If people do not have personal ownership they can feel discon-nected or even deskilled. The twin issues raised are those of personal engagement and recognition. Project ownership means control over strategic direction. It has the potential to enhance professional standing. Creative success for most people can be measured in two ways: end user value and peer recognition. For many, peer recogni-tion is the most important. People value the assessment of peers highly. We would argue that project ownership and personal creative control increases the potential for positive acknowledgement and attachment to successful projects.

The problem facing many organisations is that genuine owner-ship is often difficult to deliver due to timescales and the need for creative people to work flexibly. It is far easier to achieve with smaller projects with relatively short lives, than with those that may last 12 months or more. However, perceived lack of ownership leads to reduced levels of trust, high levels of frustration and a reduction in commitment and motivation. Such a situation is often taken to signal that senior management do not value staff, preferring control over creativity. In this situation, most people will feel that they have little opportunity to contribute ideas, being too far removed from the decision-making centre. Not only can this feeling of lack of owner-ship have a negative impact on senior management, employee rela-tionships and motivation, it also increases the level of negativity felt towards other departments and reduces trust and cooperation.

Encourage learning and diversity

A large amount of research argues that industry-specific knowledge is necessary for creative idea generation. Most writers and practitioners agree that organisations must facilitate learning and knowledge management and, although theories vary, the main thrust of thinking focuses on taught rather than tacit knowledge. We agree that having knowledge of the subject area is essential in making connections between problems and concepts. Breadth and diversity of under-standing are also important, as they bring different perspectives to a problem and help to prevent group-think and limited incremental idea development. However, few people recognise its additional value as a trust and motivational construct, particularly in terms of communication of management commitment, fulfilment of intrinsic needs and stimulating creativity.

The majority of people we have worked with or talked to, have expressed a desire to learn, whether by formal or informal means, and feel that it is instrumental in the creative process. This need stems from a desire for self-improvement, career development, an innate desire to push at the boundaries of knowledge and the recog-nition that creativity requires both stimulation and knowledge. It is interesting to note that all the companies in this book encourage and facilitate learning and exhibit high levels of interstakeholder trust, commitment and cooperation. Some, like IDEO, have developed knowledge sharing systems, what they describe as knowledge brokering, that facilitate knowledge exchange and idea development. Whereas others like PAG, British Airways or 3M ensure staff rotate through different departments or countries, develop knowledge networks that are both real (joint conferences, seminars and work-shops) and virtual (intranets and virtual communities). The key is proactive, diverse-learning management strategies. The positive effects of such strategies appear in the form of increased breadth and depth of knowledge, higher degrees of enjoyment, improved motiva-tion and positive emotional bonds to the company.

Guessing the future

We will come back to this subject in Chapter 10 – Branding and Creativity – because we believe the process of evaluating ideas has to be connected to what the brand is and hopes to become. As Tim Brown of innovation consultancy IDEO says, 'innovation is brand driven and innovation drives the brand too'. In other words, good ideas should be driven by an in-depth understanding of the brand and the meaning behind the brand values and should also, once executed, extend the idea of the brand. This is far easier if, at the front end of the process, time and creativity has been expended on defining a brief that is insightful and opens up creative opportunity. However, in the context of this chapter and as a prelude to the next where you can see the process in action, we will outline the impor-tant aspects of acceptance and rejection.

If we have been true to Linus Pauling's exhortation and if we have been good at defining a clear brief at the outset, we will at a certain point have generated a lot of seemingly good ideas. However, we know that resources are limited and at some point we need to narrow down and focus on the 'great' ideas. This potentially creates disappointment. Some people will have invested pride and commit-ment in projects and will at this point see them disappear. The only ways of mitigating this are: by ensuring that there is clarity at the beginning so that employees are aware of the judgement criteria; by providing early and good feedback on rejected ideas; and by ensuring active participation in the prototyping of ideas, so that there is self-discovery of weaknesses. The evaluation criteria will be different in each case. At Quiksilver, IDEO and Aardman the process is largely based on an intuitive feel for the brand, whereas at Funcom, PAG and Glyndebourne the creativity champions determine what works, based on issues such as timing, viability and customer input. Generally, the important attributes here are:

■ timing

■ viability

■ internal commitment/barriers

■ customer appeal

■ trust.

Timing

When an organisation is dealing with creative ideas, it is trying to define a largely unknown future. The question then has to be asked, whether the time is right for an idea. In his very entertaining book about Silicon Valley, *Accidental Empires*, Robert X Cringely (1996) narrates the experiences of Xerox PARC and the development of the Alto computer. The computer scientists who developed this product in the early seventies created the first workstation. They went where no one else had gone. The Alto had built-in networking using Ethernet, a bit-mapped screen, a mouse and hard-disk data storage. In fact, all the things we would expect of a workstation today. But this was 1973. Cringely notes that it was 'a wonder, but it wasn't a product' (p83). It would have cost about $25,000, making it about $22,000 too expensive and it lacked a compelling application. The Alto (and Ethernet) was an idea whose time hadn't come. In generating ideas that confront the forefront of technology, evaluation needs to be rigorous and based on a strong understanding of customer needs.

Viability

In brainstorming processes the emphasis is on being non-judgemental. Any idea is OK. However, afterwards ideas need to be reviewed. While we should avoid the dangers of group-think and question real or imagined barriers, we also need to be realistic to ensure that ideas are realisable. This is a difficult process. We cannot question all our assumptions, because every assumption contains another one, but we need to question what Flaubert called 'received ideas'.[3] A critical, questioning voice is vital, as is a realistic assessment of the organisation's ability to deliver what is suggested. As Aardman's executive producer Miles Bullough notes:

> You have to talk to them [animators] as openly and honestly as you can. Creative people are sensitive and you can't just go tramping all over their idea. Remember they are putting something of themselves out there ... Your job is to get rid of the debris and select the ideas. It's about getting people not to be too precious about ideas, you have to be able to say to them, 'no, that's crap let's work on this one, build it up and polish it until it's really good. Remember it's only an idea' ... Again it's about getting them to see what they are good at and forget about what they would like to be. My job as a creative manager is helping them see what they are good at. Help fulfil them and limit frustration.
>
> *(Interview with author dated 15 July 2003)*

Internal commitment/barriers

The more mainstream an idea the greater the chance of acceptance and commitment. This is not to suggest that non-mainstream ideas should be ignored but it will always be harder to convince senior management to support revolutionary ideas. The implication of this in the assessment process is that managers have to recognise that they will have to work that much harder on preparation and in presenting their case and overcoming internal barriers. This requires passion and as much focus on the internal customers as the external ones. The ability to anticipate internal objections and put forward strong arguments is often excellent preparation for launching on the market. This was certainly the case with Ken Kutaragi's campaign within Sony to develop the Playstation in spite of corporate indifference and also car designer J. Mays' attempts to overcome VW management's antipathy towards the Beetle. In the case of the latter, it pushed designer Mays to conduct extensive research and to develop a branding campaign for the car alongside the car design itself.

Customer appeal

Most organisations erect barriers between themselves and their customers: 'us' inside the organisation designing things for 'them' outside the organisation. However, companies like Quiksilver and PAG, are good at co-creating. Rather than assume that they know what customers want they involve them in the process of idea creation. IDEO practice this all the time. They eschew the idea of focused groups, but are very passionate about 'unfocused' ones. Here they work with the users of products and services to brainstorm ideas, develop prototypes and test concepts in use. Similarly, games company Funcom involve users in ongoing development of games. All these organisations feel that the often abstracted nature of formalised market research does not give the insight that close obser-vation and co-creation deliver.

Trust

In an episode of *The Simpsons*, called 'Simpson and Delilah', Homer acquires a full head of hair by taking a miracle formula. The normally bald Homer suddenly acquires a more dynamic persona and his boss Burns promotes him. Homer starts to dress differently and becomes a trusted employee – after being the longest serving junior in the company. In response to a request from Burns to reduce industrial accidents, Homer comes up with the creative idea of adding tartar sauce to the fish sticks in the canteen. Is it a good or a bad idea? Rather than listening to some hired consultants, the new Homer is a trusted figure, so the idea is implemented and indeed acci-dents do fall. As a result Homer earns the key to the executive wash-room. Of course, the real reason accidents fall is that Homer, with his promotion, is no longer in the canteen causing them.[4] The moral of this story is that trust is a requirement for carrying an idea in an organisation. As we will see in the case of Aardman and Funcom in the next chapter, trust has to be earned through action.

Feedback

The final point to note is that quality feedback is required throughout the course of a project. Whether this is positive or negative, the key to success here is in the empathy and skills of the manager, or 'emotional intelligence'. The manager has first to recognise the importance of communication and then deliver it effectively on a regular basis. Enthusiasm and passion should come through, but hype should be avoided. Employees can often see through exaggerated claims and consequently become cynical and sometimes when the hype is believed it makes negative information emotionally difficult to handle. As previously noted, one of the key ways to maintain trust is to ensure that when promises are made they are kept. An example of this process in action is the case of Siemens-Nixdorf, where an open process was fundamental to building trust and involvement. Siemens-Nixdorf was the company formed as a result of the acquisition of Nixdorf by Siemens in 1990. From the beginning the company had problems and for four years it cut staff, failed to find a new corporate direction and bled money, accumulating losses of DM2 billion. Not surprisingly morale was low. Then in 1994 a new CEO arrived. He decided to engage everyone in the company in a new turnaround programme. He provided people with an honest review of the business, stated clearly how future decisions would be made and then asked for employees to come up with ideas to help transform the company. After three months, 405 people had contributed their opinions and ideas. Eventually 9000 people had made suggestions. To ensure that good ideas led to action, the suggestions were then auctioned to executives who took responsibility for implementation. Inevitably some ideas were rejected, but importantly the process was seen as fair. By 1995 employee satisfaction had nearly doubled and the company was in the black.

In stark contrast is the case of VW, where the management of a plant in Puebla, Mexico offered a new labour agreement to its employees that featured a 20% pay rise. Although the sum was generous it led to a walkout and a prolonged industrial dispute. The offer itself was more than fair, but the lack of discussion and participation led to mistrust and disappointment (Chan and Mauborgne 2003).

Conclusion

To experiment and express their individuality within a stable organisational framework, employees need autonomy. However, this is not a recipe for chaos – such a framework should consist of both explicit and implicit boundaries. It is essential that people are not told what to do but are told what not to do, in the broadest terms. The development of such frameworks might be seen to go against more traditional views of creativity management, but our case companies illustrate that both focus and business direction are key to providing an environment in which employees can concentrate on creativity without distraction or fear. Clarity is key. In addition to this support we suggest that employees be given reasonable power and control over their work to ensure a positive sense of project ownership. If people believe they are just acting in a supplier role, feeling that their input is not valued or that they have no personal involvement in a project, intrinsic motivation declines and they will become frustrated and resentful of management.

We identified in Chapter 2 that the recruitment of employees with the right abilities, attitudes and values is important in developing creative cultures and that the building of trust stems initially from leadership-led strategies and values. The overall aim of managers should be the development of a protective, supportive, yet commercially focused environment that can deliver the required levels of personal support and understanding within a framework designed to deliver competitive value. The model in Figure 4.1 illustrates this concept showing how key leadership abilities and characteristics provide such an environment by exhibiting emotional intelligence and delivering resources, support and direction.

The outer ring of the model represents the essential emotional intelligence requirements that successful leaders of creative people have and exhibit. They provide the initial supportive constructs that form the basis of a creative culture. Within this shell, managers can then deliver more specific constructs that fulfil both creative and

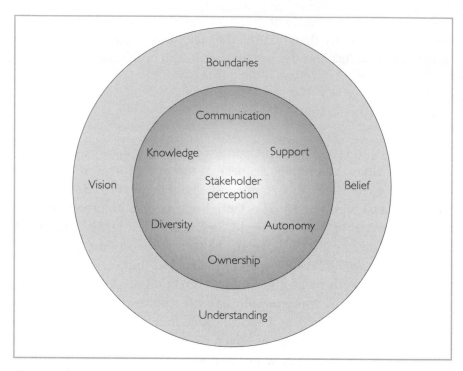

Figure 4.1 The supportive model of creative leadership

commercial needs. At the heart of this system are the stakeholders and it is their perception of managers' ability to deliver these constructs that determine levels of trust between stakeholders and the nature of relationships. For such an environment to be sustained, managers must act in a mentoring role, with the focus on understanding, developing and supporting staff, rather than controlling them. Such a coaching style of management relies on a high level of emotional intelligence that balances personal freedom with commercial need. Our work highlights the idea that employees want managers to provide a safe but challenging environment, which supports, educates and inspires, while still allowing them the freedom to experiment and challenge perceived norms. Successful mentoring can help give focus and improve knowledge; it can also generate the perception of an environment that is safe and supportive of creative risk taking. It is important that managers achieve the correct balance between support and freedom. If they are perceived to be too controlling, they can smother creativity by limiting trust. However, passive mentoring may lead to frustration, lack of focus, and the perception that management is either incompetent or does not care about outputs or employees.

At the heart of the concept is an understanding that the majority of employees within today's knowledge-based economy are highly trained, intrinsically motivated people who are very sensitive to social environments. Traditional attempts to control or implement extrinsically based reward schemes often increase conflict, as well as reducing trust and cooperation. It is therefore important that managers show that they trust staff to behave in a professional manner by granting them the autonomy and information to experiment and express their individuality within an agreed organisational framework. We believe that such a framework can be viewed as an informal contract promoting self-regulation. However, it is important that such frameworks do not reduce employees' perception of project ownership.

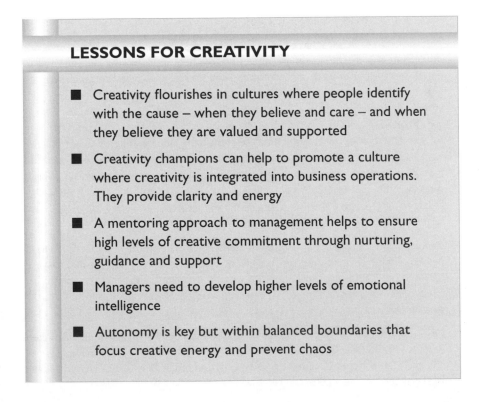

LESSONS FOR CREATIVITY

■ Creativity flourishes in cultures where people identify with the cause – when they believe and care – and when they believe they are valued and supported

■ Creativity champions can help to promote a culture where creativity is integrated into business operations. They provide clarity and energy

■ A mentoring approach to management helps to ensure high levels of creative commitment through nurturing, guidance and support

■ Managers need to develop higher levels of emotional intelligence

■ Autonomy is key but within balanced boundaries that focus creative energy and prevent chaos

- Commitment is also heightened through a strong sense of project ownership and a focus on intrinsic motivators

- Creativity needs diversity of knowledge. Managers must resource and encourage a breadth of formal and informal learning strategies

- Ongoing honest yet sensitive feedback is vital in maintaining enthusiasm for creativity

Notes

1   Xerox PARC has been much written about, because it was the place where personal computing was developed and it spawned a whole series of businesses that commercialised the IT business. It invented the laser printer, the computer network, double-click technology and perfected the graphical user interface, but none of it benefited Xerox. Palo Alto is a long way geographically and psychologically from upstate New York (Xerox's head office) and Xerox always saw itself as the copier company – not a computer company. The opportunities were ignored and Adobe, Apple and Microsoft reaped the rewards.

2   This thinking ties in with that of Frederick Herzberg (2003) who has observed that satisfaction and dissatisfaction are not opposites but relate to two sets of human needs: the built-in drive to avoid pain and the desire to experience psychological growth. The factors that contribute to job satisfaction are primarily to do with the latter and consist of achievement, recognition, the work itself, responsibility and growth or advancement. The factors that contribute to dissatisfaction are primarily the former and consist of interpersonal relationships, supervision, company policy, working conditions, salary, status and security. To achieve fulfilment, employees need to have their work enriched by motivational elements, such as removing controls (while retaining accountability), granting additional authority and providing direct feedback. Trying to engage employees through what Herzberg calls 'hygiene factors', such as salary and status, is to misunderstand people's relationship to their jobs.

3   Flaubert's satirical *Dictionary of Received Ideas* (cited in de Botton 2002, pp79–82) described the French bourgeoisie's prejudices, such as 'architects: all idiots; they always forget to put staircases in houses; English women: express surprise that they can have pretty children; French: the greatest people in the world; Italians: all musical. All treacherous.'

4   Originally aired on 18 October 1990, the episode has been analysed by Czarniawska, Barbara and Rhodes, Carl in 'Strong Plots: the relationship between popular culture and management practice and theory'. Paper presented at The Role of Humanities in the Formation of New European Elites, Venice 10–12 September 2003.

Aardman and Funcom

Animated creativity

5

The most important thing is, we have to work as a team.
Which means that you do everything I tell you.

Rocky, The Flying Rooster

The issue that Rocky raises in Aardman's animated feature film, *Chicken Run*,[1] is how to best manage creativity. In any project of scale there is always the challenge of how to involve, excite and maintain the enthusiasm of a diverse collection of people. This is especially true when the projects are long term, highly detailed and founded on the vision of one individual. It requires clear direction, but also participation. It requires continuous creativity, but also control. And it requires trust, which makes Rocky's ironic statement about teams, particularly apposite. The task he is setting to a group of chickens is to learn to fly, which of course he knows to be impossible. The chickens believe that Rocky can fly (and thus that they can as well) because one of them has seen him shooting through the air – although the reality is that he is a circus performer who has been fired from a cannon. But the chickens' desire to escape from their farm, before they get turned into chicken pies, encourages them to believe in the chimera of flight. Rocky manipulates this desire, not through genuine teamwork (which might expose him) but through control. Here, the chickens' hopes are misplaced and their faith goes unrewarded. However, later in the film, there is a moment of genuine teamwork, when the chickens seize the opportunity to build an aeroplane. The moment of inspiration is a casual one, but the vision of powered flight galvanises the chickens to achieve something that seems unrealisable. They become highly resourceful (aided by two rats), courageous and involved. They steal the farmer's tools and clothes from under his nose; they create detailed plans for the 'old crate'; and they work collectively, under pressure to make a primitive flying machine. Rather than Rocky's dictatorial style, the leading character among the chickens, Ginger, is encouraging and nurturing. She keeps the main objective in front of the chickens, pushes them when she needs to but allows them to use their own creativity.

As the previous chapter indicates it is Ginger's mentoring style that seems to be most valuable in encouraging creativity. This chapter will narrate the way two organisations do this: the Bristol-based animated film-makers Aardman who created *Wallace and Gromit*, *Creature Comforts* and *Chicken Run* and Funcom, the Norwegian online game developers and producers of 'Anarchy Online' and 'The Longest Journey'.

Leading creativity

The fences aren't just around the farm. They're up here, in your heads.

Ginger

One of Ginger's roles is creativity champion. She urges her fellow chickens to think of new ways of escaping the farm and she paints a picture of a better place where there are wide open spaces, trees and green grass. However, many of her fellow chickens are cynics and most are constrained by their inability to imagine a world other than the one they live in. One tells her that the chances of escape are a million to one, to which Ginger replies with seemingly unbounded optimism, 'there's still a chance then'. Most of Ginger's attempts at escape are individualistic and mirror Steve McQueen's attempts in *The Great Escape*, from which *Chicken Run* takes its inspiration; inevitably they're doomed to fail. When Ginger manages to persuade the other chickens of her vision the escape is achieved as a collective effort. The relationships between the chickens and the approach to creativity is a metaphor for Aardman itself.

Originally started in 1972 by two school friends, Peter Lord and David Sproxton, Aardman's international fame rests primarily on its Oscar©-winning films based on the Plasticine characters, Wallace and Gromit. These films, and indeed *Chicken Run*, were ideas dreamt up by the animator Nick Park, whom Peter and David recruited from the National Film and Television School. The first Wallace and Gromit film, *A Grand Day Out* was Park's graduation film, but after five years of study, he'd only managed six minutes of film. With Aardman's support and structure Park finished the film in 1989. Two further films followed; *The Wrong Trousers* (1994) and *A Close Shave* (1996). As the scale of the films developed, so did the nature of creativity and the requirement to manage the process. While the first film was largely an individual effort by Park, *The Wrong Trousers* used 5 animators. For *A Close Shave* the budget was £1.3 million (double the previous film) and required yet more animators, while *Chicken Run* had 25 animators and 180 people in total working on the project. This transition from individual hobbyist film maker to director of a team changed Park's role in the film process. While he was still involved in the animation, his core role became idea writer/director and creativity champion. David Sproxton, executive chairman describes it as follows:

> If you take Nick Park, he has more than one good idea, but what we do with him is give him a small team of like-minded people who will help look for ideas. There are people like the writer Bob Baker. He works with Nick and is literally fishing for ideas ... Bob is great at saying to Nick, this is a great idea, but this one is less strong. The job is to get rid of the debris and select the ideas. It's about getting people not to be too precious.
>
> *(Interview with author dated 15 July 2003)*

Sproxton and executive producer, Miles Bullough, see their role as minders, gatekeepers and editors, who are able to get staff to see what they are good at and forget about what they would like to be. As Bullough went on to note:

> My job as a creative manager is helping them [creatives] see what they are good at. Help fulfil them and limit frustration ... We just have to try and be there to

support them if they haven't driven you insane. It's like being a parent in many ways, you have to let them make their own mistakes and hope they don't do themselves serious damage.

(Interview with author dated 15 July 2003)

They recognise the need to create a supportive environment where people trust each other and where individuals can take risks. They believe in providing guidance and direction that supports staff rather than restricts them. This allows Park and others to be challengingly surreal.

It could be argued that Aardman is a one off, but the other company that features in this chapter, Funcom, exhibits many of the same traits. This company was started in 1993 in Oslo by a group of people who were passionate about creating games. Like Sproxton and Lord's start-up, the founders had no real business experience and no directly relevant academic training. But they did have ideas and within two years there were 100 people in the company. Within Funcom, game ideas tend to be developed by a core group of people. Gaute Godager, one of the founders and a game director, believes that ideas could potentially come from anywhere in the company, but that practically it tends to be three or four people who develop the original vision. His argument is that to carry an idea you need a track record:

You need to have trust from management and it needs to have the backing of the people who are going to work on it. It's so much to do with trust, which is why so few people do the original concept.

(Interview with author dated 17 March 2003)

Indeed, Godager argues that generating ideas is not the real challenge. In the hothouse environment of Funcom, where the designers and programmers are themselves passionate games players, game ideas are circulating all the time. The difficulty is to decide which ideas are most interesting. His role as game director is to assess ideas against an intuitive feel for what will connect with the playing audience, the requirements of the company's strategic plan and the best revenue opportunity. Although there can be no guarantee that the right choices are made, the strength of the people at Funcom (and also at Aardman) is the close connection to their customers. As with the example of Quiksilver in Chapter 9, if the members of the organisation are also the customers, the quality of decision making should be stronger. It also builds confidence and enables these organisations to have the courage to do the unexpected.

For example, the idea of *The Great Escape* with chickens set in a 1950s northern England farm might appear worryingly eccentric to most people, yet the film is the third highest grossing British film ever in the US (2002) (www.aardman.com). Equally, amidst the empire building and warfare genres that dominate games playing, Funcom's 'The Longest Journey' (1997) was a courageous choice. It draws on the idea of strong themes and the difficulty of confronting complex moral choices. In the game, the central character is an 18-year-old girl called April Ryan, who has a dead-end job with a bad boss, a small apartment with no air conditioning and an uninspiring and pestering admirer. While the game has external action and features travel between parallel worlds, the title actually refers to the inner journey of April Ryan to find personal meaning. The appeal of the game, lies in the way it tackles existential problems in an imaginative futuristic context. Godager argues that the game, with its internal dialogues and self-questioning, also has a Woody Allen feel to it. Although 'The Longest Journey' is outside the norm for a computer game, it has also been a critical and commercial success.[2]

Creativity meets reality

In the worlds of Aardman and Funcom, the willingness to create derives from the passion of people, the need of individuals to express their creativity and the desire for peer applause. The cultures are supportive and courageous. This is important in encouraging ideas, enabling them to be rejected without undermining the self-belief of people or given enthusiastic support if they feel right. Bullough summed up the views of both companies reflecting:

> You have to talk to them [creatives] as openly and honestly as you can. Creative people are sensitive and you can't just go tramping all over their idea. Remember they are putting something of themselves out there.
>
> *(Interview with author dated 15 July 2003)*

For example, it would have been all too easy to misjudge the quirky idea of *The Wrong Trousers*. Imagine trying to evaluate this concept: the story features a cheese-loving inventor (Wallace) and his knowing dog (Gromit). The inventor develops a pair of high-tech trousers, which are hijacked by a penguin (who has become a tenant of the inventor) in a robbery. The inventor and dog manage to retrieve the stolen goods and the penguin is arrested. The idea has Cocteau-like shifts in the nature of reality and the story puts forward an interesting dilemma about trust, but has it got commercial legs? As we have seen these judgements are based on a feeling and whether the idea ends up being successful is a lot to do with the way the idea is developed. There are sometimes seemingly interesting concepts that fail in their execution and equally, prosaic concepts that end up exciting. Citing the thinking of the existential psychologist and writer Rollo May, Godager says:

> He said creativity isn't chaos. Creativity isn't structure. Creativity isn't ideas. Creativity is to let chaos meet structure. That is where creativity is found. To me that's really true … It's not the idea itself, it's the meeting with reality, which is true creativity.[3]
>
> *(Interview with author dated 17 March 2003)*

The sorts of projects that Aardman and Funcom deliver are complex and long term. Funcom's most recent high-profile creation is 'Anarchy Online': it took 40 people four years to complete and an investment of $10 million. Aardman's *Chicken Run* involved 180 people over 18 months to generate 80 minutes of film with development and preproduction adding a further three years. The detail of these projects means that there are continuous opportunities for creativity as well as the potential for boredom and creative stagnation to set in. This is creativity at the most detailed level. In the preproduction phase, the emphasis is on honing the idea. As Sproxton says:

> Mostly it's rejection; paring things down and focusing the idea. We are going through the same thing with the Wallace and Gromit film. Mostly you are chucking stuff out and getting people to accept it's not working.
>
> *(Interview with author dated 15 July 2003)*

During development work, there has to be an open and honest dialogue between what is seen to work and what doesn't. Aardman's experience is that it is the chemistry between team members that ensures there is trust as the creative vision evolves. Once the vision is encoded into the storyboard, the boundaries of creativity become narrower, but it is often the subtleties that are introduced during filming that surprise and entertain. Here the input of team members is vital. For example, each animator has to take the 18-inch model of a particular character and animate one frame at a time. At a rate of 24 frames per second, the animator has to imagine how to convey movement or emotion in slow motion. If characters speak, there is a further complexity, because the mouth has to be replaced after each syllable. This is painstakingly slow work and produces, on average, less than 10 seconds of film per week, per animator; although an ensemble piece where there is a lot of interaction takes much longer. While there is creativity in the animation of characters, it is the combination of sets (with their expressionistic feel), voice-overs, sound effects and music that creates a plausible and engaging story. The whole process relies on 'chaos and structure'.

Funcom's processes share many of the same principles as Aardman, but the development process appears looser and also more connected to customers. Godager argues that although you have an idea of how to do things when you start, you don't know exactly where you will end up. The idea will evolve as the various specialists input their thoughts while the actions of competitors sometimes dictate shifts in direction. Equally, because the process is inexact, Godager also believes it's very hard to know when you're finished. From a creative perspective, the tendency is to keep going to perfect the game, while from a financial perspective, deadlines need to be set and met. The former can be seen in those films and games that extend and extend their deadlines (and budgets). Funcom experienced the latter with 'Anarchy Online' when commercial pressures dictated a launch before the game was sufficiently well developed, which led to disappointed customers and remedial work to improve the player experience. Dealing with this type of uncertainty is a fundamental part of creative management. While the guiding framework of the idea can define the boundaries of development, there is no tick box method for determining the relevance of different inputs. This means that the creativity champion needs to balance direction with freedom. Within Funcom, the initial idea will evolve into a scenario that all the key people from different disciplines take part in. They are trying to imagine the player experience, the sequences of logic and the quality of interaction. Once the overall scenario is in place, various specialists such as game designers, concept artists and music people work sequentially in teams. However, they also come together to ensure that overlaps between the disciplines are managed and the designs go through various prototyping stages to check that the concept is working. Once the prototype is agreed, the programming work begins. While the perception is that programming is a technical discipline, in reality it is a creative process. No two programmers will work in exactly the same way; they will see ideas and tackle problems from different perspectives. Thus the process from beginning to end has a requirement for creative input, which needs to be managed. Unstructured creativity would lead to anarchy and the loss of the original vision. The evolution of the original idea is defined by the leaders in the various disciplines and ultimately the game director. And also by the input from customers. As Godager says:

> When you're done, you're not done at all. You need player feedback – that will change the game several times. We also need to go through quality assurance. So, you quickly become blind to your own designs. That sense of experiencing a game for the first time, you can only have once, but you need to get that feeling back, because the first 30 minutes of game playing is the most crucial. That's why you need to have new people coming in to focus test your product all the time. So you have a concept that's delivered by a few and then it's taken on by a lot of experts in their fields. One person – that's me – has to be responsible for making sure that the input from the specialists works for the team.[4]
>
> *(Interview with author dated 17 March 2003)*

What is quite explicit in both the Aardman and Funcom processes is that creativity is seen as 'the sum of all the little things you do'. To achieve this both companies try to recruit people with high levels of skill in their specific disciplines. This is important because the project team members need to have trust in the capability of each other and because no one person can micromanage the detail. In these companies it is the senior managers' role to inspire people about the animation or game idea and to set the boundaries of creativity. In Funcom's case Godager knows he doesn't have the technical expertise to oversee the specifics, so employees are allowed as much creative freedom as they can prove they can deal with. The value is that the individual team members feel a very strong sense of project ownership – it is their individual and collective creativity that defines the game. Partly, this is an issue of scale. Whereas a company like Disney can employ highly specialist individuals who do key frames and nothing else, Funcom and Aardman need people who can cover bigger areas and input their creativity into the detail. Partly this is also an issue of philosophy; a view that the ability to express creativity is fulfilling. Godager says:

> It's the belief in the game that leads people to put in the extra effort, which is why people management is actually creative management. You have to make sure that people believe in it [the game] and that they want to unlock their creativity.
>
> *(Interview with author dated 17 March 2003)*

Not surprisingly, the level of intrinsic motivation in both companies is high. There is a strong sense of engagement and pride in the project, the work environment and the team. The strong sense of team is also driven by the feeling of a hostile external environment. Each team wants to create a great game or film – one that will create peer and customer appreciation – but it also feels the pressure to perform. The problem the manager faces in this context is coping with the ambition of the game designers or animators, who, as observed earlier, always want to make the best game or film ever. However, time and budgets never allow this nirvana, so the reality is that the scope has to be narrowed and cut. This is always a difficult decision and one that needs to fall to the producer or director who is responsible for maintaining the vision.

Difficult choices

While both Aardman and Funcom are able to generate high levels of identification with projects and create a sense of ownership through giving people the freedom to create, there are also difficult choices to make. These choices involve three linked areas: team membership, creative evolution and maintenance of the vision.

First, getting the members of the team right is seen as vital. As well as having the technical skills so that the team feels it has the potential to deliver an excellent product, the chemistry also needs to work. The latter point is stressed by Aardman because they feel that the cohesion of the team can easily be undermined by personal conflict. Sproxton cites the example of a TV series, where the technical ability was in place, but the group became disfunctional. Aardman decided that the original idea was strong, but that the vision of it could only be realised with a different team.

Within Funcom, the focus of team members is primarily with the game they are developing. Individuals are motivated to deliver the best within their specific remit, but they also need to connect with other team members whose skills may fall into a radically different area. A visual artist who is creating a fantasy world set 30,000 years in the future has to connect with a software engineer, whose primary concern is how the programming will work. Both have to be willing and capable to learn from each other and to solve problems together without reducing efficiency. In describing the culture of Funcom, Godager says:

> Innovative, self-examining (not taking anything for granted), cooperative and teamwork. Everyone says they work in teams, but we're 110% dependent on teams. For a product to work there needs to be one person in each area who knows what's going on. There needs to be creative discipline, but within that framework there needs to be a lot of freedom. Meeting those two demands is quite difficult: we need people to be involved as early as possible to make sure the details work. But we don't need them to be like a committee.
>
> *(Interview with author dated 17 March 2003)*

Second, Funcom's and Aardman's projects are marathons not sprints. When a project stretches across several years, enthusiasm needs to be maintained and creativity needs to be nurtured. At Aardman there is a conscious policy of change to keep the team fresh and focused. New people come into the group and some people are switched around. Bullough argues that as the project evolves there are new challenges that emerge. Although the company has learned stop frame animation techniques over a number of years, there are always new requirements that haven't been encountered before: such as how to communicate the idea of a chicken thinking by changing its body shape; how to create a believable impression of chickens flying. It is the daily confrontation with the difficulties of animation that help encourage ongoing innovation. Although Nick Park is puzzled by the question of slow pace – he thinks it moves very quickly – others need the reassurance of collective progress. To achieve this, the shooting schedule of an animated film such as *Chicken Run* is divided up into

10-week phases. This gives people more achievable goals than trying to paint a picture of what will be in place after 18 months of shooting. When each phase is complete the work is reviewed and celebrated. At Funcom the levels of motivation are maintained within the team by similar mechanisms, with the importance of communication being stressed. Like Sproxton, Godager argues that while there are high levels of self-motivation because of the passion people bring to their jobs, they also need supporting through the difficult periods. He believes that this isn't about hype, which they see through anyway, but about reassuring the team by giving them information about what competitors are doing, the way the market is evolving and why the game in development is going to be 'cool and successful'.

Third, there is the difficult balance of maintaining the integrity of the original vision of the game or film, while allowing creative freedom during development. Manage too tightly and creative opportunities will be missed and people will feel less involved. Manage too loosely and the original vision can be lost. The director and creative guardian of the vision needs to manage this balance. This will mean difficult decisions have to be made. In Aardman, the vision is the responsibility of the director, while the producer manages the project. In Funcom, the combined roles are largely the responsibility of the game director. In both cases, ideas and suggestions have to be encouraged but rejection also needs to be handled and people pushed to maximise their potential. This requires the qualities detailed in the previous chapter: self-awareness, empathy, trustworthy behaviour and social skills. It means that team members have to trust the creative leaders to act with integrity and in the best interests of the creative content of the game or film. The more difficult scenario is where the producer or game director has to make decisions not because of creative considerations but because of commercial imperative. Whereas the team may be fully supportive of the former, because their primary concern is peer applause, they are generally not so motivated by strategic or financial considerations. Within Aardman, Sproxton says, there is often a resistance to the marketing or business view, while Godager notes:

> I'm one of the most controversial people at Funcom ... I have a feel for what the product needs to be, to be able to compete. I sense people get angry with me. I'm the one who has to say to people, this doesn't work – cut it out.
>
> (Interview with author dated 17 March 2003)

Conclusion

Aardman and Funcom benefit from passionate, motivated and highly skilled employees. However, all this commitment counts for nothing if there is a lack of focus. What we can observe in these organisations is that visionary individuals, who have built up the trust of employees through a proven track record, can give films or games clear leadership and inspire their team members. While we might imagine from the outside that the visionary is a solo creative individual, the creativity of an Aardman film or a Funcom game is very much a collective effort. Success is defined in part by the originality of an idea, but the real connection to the audience and the overall creativity is very much defined by all the small creative acts and decisions taken during the development process. It is this that defines the appeal of the characters. As Sproxton says, 'you can't plan loveable characters or the universal appeal'. In management terms, the real challenge is to get the balance right between setting the creative framework and then allowing people freedom to develop their own ideas. Where you end up may not always be where you intended to go, but the hope is that the final result is better, both creatively and commercially.

LESSONS FOR CREATIVITY

- Creativity does need visionary individuals, but more importantly it needs highly motivated and involved teams

- Although some organisations micromanage the execution of ideas, this denies the opportunity for individuals to contribute their own creative ideas; it is far better to use the full intellectual capital you have at your disposal as long as it is focused by creative frameworks

- Individuals are motivated to perform largely by intrinsic factors and can become strongly connected to projects in which they feel a sense of ownership

- While organisations imagine that creativity is in the original idea, these examples suggest that much of the creativity that really connects with audiences derives from many creative decisions in the implementation process

- Managers need to build a trusting environment where people feel they can take risks and challenge the accepted ways of doing things; this is about mentoring based on a knowledge of team members

Notes

1   For more on *Chicken Run* (2000), see www.aardman.com and www.chickenrun.co.uk.

2   'The Longest Journey' has sold 400,000 units (www.gameindustry.com 2002) and has received many critical plaudits. Take for example the following from GiN: 'This is hands down the best adventure game currently on the market. It overcomes its minor flaws with a sheer beauty that simply can't be matched.' For more press coverage see www.funcom.com.

3   For a complementary idea of the creative act as an ongoing, detailed process, take this definition of Jean Cocteau's creativity, 'ultimately the creative act – the poetry in Cocteau's understanding of the word – is above all a question of working, crafting, putting together, making, in the Greek sense of the word, *poiesis*.' *Jean Cocteau Sur le fil du siècle*, Centre Pompidou, 2003.

4   Henry Mintzberg argues that there is a belief that strategy is somehow disconnected from process and that there is also a myth about the heroic leader as innovator. He says, 'to be innovative requires the freedom to act, in places where the detailed knowledge is held. Complex innovation also requires that the action be collective, in free-flowing teamwork.' Mintzberg, Henry 'Managing to Innovate' in *Leading for Innovation* (2002) (ed.) Hesselbein, Frances, Goldsmith, Marshall and Somerville, Iain p142. Jossey-Bass, San Francisco.

6 Balancing Act

Designing and managing creative teams

We live in a world of organisations. Our opportunity to express our creativity is consequently constrained by the needs of the organisation and its accountability to customers and shareholders. We also live in a social world where we must work with others and share ideas. As Carl Jung (1993) says, 'I need we to be fully I.' So, when we're part of a team our opportunity for unbridled creativity is again constrained – this time by the pressure and differing viewpoints of colleagues. Frustrating? It can be, especially if you're an individualist. Yet this constraint is not necessarily negative, because what organisations should also do is provide resources, support and direction. They make dreams realisable. Similarly, the other members of a creative team should provide us with inspiration and energy. So the way we should really evaluate an organisation and a team is how well it contributes to the freedom of all parties. This turns our role as a team participant on its head. Rather than a narrow idea of our own personal freedom, we must think about the freedom we are helping to create not only for ourselves but also for people both inside and outside the organisation. As the philosopher Peter Koestenbaum says (Koestenbaum and Block 2001),

The ideals of human perfectibility and of achievement are authentic antidotes to the existential anxiety of guilt. What is true

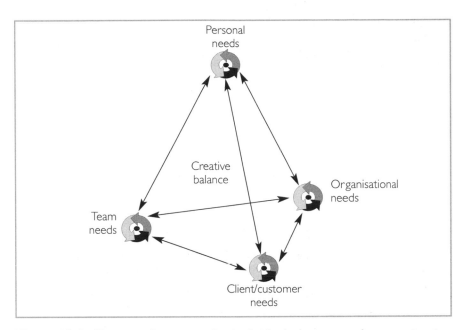

Personal
needs

Creative
balance

Organisational
needs

Team
needs

Client/customer
needs

Figure 6.1 Tensions between the individual, the team, the organisation and the customer

for an individual is also true for our institutions. This understanding of existential guilt will ultimately lead us to measure all institutions – such as a business, the family, education, the law, commerce and politics – by the degree to which they support the development of human potential. (p314)

A thought that is also echoed by the Nobel Prize winning economist, Amartya Sen (1999, p142), who says, 'Not only do institutions contribute to our freedoms, their roles can be sensibly evaluated in the light of their contributions to our freedom.' The implication of this desire for freedom is that there needs to be a balance between the competing needs for different sorts of freedom. If one need dominates over others then imbalance occurs and creative potential is reduced. Figure 6.1 illustrates the internal and external tensions that exist between the individual, the team, the organisation and the customer. Not only does each need apply pressure to the others, but as we will see with the examples in the following chapters, the needs themselves are also volatile. For, just as everything seems in balance, something changes: the organisation moves the project deadline or the client rewrites the brief. This chapter investigates the problem of achieving equilibrium between competing needs and discusses how various pressures can affect the tensions within the team and creative relationships.

Designing creative teams

A creative team is a microcosm of the organisation. It should, therefore, exhibit similar characteristics and balance the need for order with that for self-expression. Of course, this is an ideal. Many organisations are hierarchically based and self-expression is looked down upon or even regarded as dangerous. Daniel Ellsberg (2002) gives an example of this in his book on the Vietnam War. He advised Secretary of Defense McNamara and subsequently released the Pentagon papers, which showed the extent of government and military myopia about Vietnam. He describes the prevailing philosophy in successive government administrations as:

> Do what's good for your boss, the man who hired you; put that above what you think is best for your country, above giving the president or the secretary of defense your best advice if that would embarrass your boss. *(p53)*

What normally happens in these repressive environments is that personal freedom, the willingness to take risks and trust all diminish, while demotivation, conflict, political action and lack of cooperation increase. If Ellsberg's view reflects behaviour in governments generally, we should not be surprised if political thinking lacks creativity. However, we should also be wary of overly informal structures where there is little constraint on self-expression. This is well illustrated in William Golding's (1997[1954]) novel *Lord of the Flies*, which tells the story of a group of air-wrecked schoolboys and their descent from civilisation to savagery. The core theme of the book is that it is the ideals, values, and structures of society that determine the success of a community. We can observe that without adequate direction in a team it is sometimes only a small step to autarchy or anarchy with people feeling vulnerable, confused, isolated and oscillating between defensive and aggressive behaviour.

Successful self-management can only occur when the needs of the individual and the team are aligned and where trust exists. Without a supportive structure it is likely that stronger or more dominant individuals will take control of a group, preventing such alignment. Team members then revert either to controlling behaviour or they lose focus and motivation. Without structure, teams will not be effective decision makers and will tend to suffer from a lack of direction because personal desires dominate. At first sight this may appear to run against the grain of the literature and contemporary thinking that advocates high levels of team autonomy. However, our research confirms that structure and direction are required for meaningful autonomy to occur.

While there needs to be personal freedom in a team, support from outside helps to establish trust, goals and responsibilities. This does not necessarily mean that a single omnipotent team leader or board director directs decision making and idea generation. The leader's role should primarily be that of inspirer and mentor. Nor do we believe that highly specific role responsibilities for team members are necessary as this can pigeonhole people's talents and discourage diversity and motivation. People may have hidden abilities that are obscured by their primary roles: we can sometimes be surprised by the creativity of a banker (Paul Gauguin), a civil servant (Henri Rousseau) or an insurance clerk (Franz Kafka). In an attempt to overcome a lack of knowledge about individuals, managers often resort to Belbin's (1993) model of role designation to achieve a balanced team. However, we would argue that it is too simplistic to rely on this to assign role personalities and jobs. Overreliance on such a model reduces group flexibility by imposing preset perceptions of how individuals should act and by imposing boundaries on them in terms of responsibilities and input. Consequently this can reduce insight and encourage the formation of traditionally based power relationships.

What we argue for is simple supportive structures that reinforce key organisational objectives and systems and define broad spans of responsibility for team members. Simple structures act as flexible templates, allowing team members to enjoy freedom within specified constraints, while also stimulating senior management confidence and trust. This achieves a balance between the needs and tensions of the different audiences: diversity of thinking within a common framework of core values, objectives and systems. This is good for relationships within the group and encourages respect and trust with outsiders. Thus, while structure helps to define core boundaries and responsibilities, it is the team's ability to work together that makes the creative process succeed (or not). In this ideal, no interest dominates and each party contributes to stimulating creativity. Team members feel positive about themselves and the role of the team and focus their efforts on delivering benefits. Individual roles and boundaries are understood and respected, as are limitations and needs, and the team shows good balance. Finally, team members exhibit vision clarity (ability to articulate objectives) and shared vision (ability to pool and negotiate ideas), which helps them to act in a collaborative, focused and creative manner.

Size and diversity

There is a commonly held view that a small team made up of diversely experienced people helps facilitate creativity. This is certainly the route taken by such organisations as IDEO, Design Bridge, Funcom and Tate Modern. The development of more socially based informal interaction is more likely to occur in small teams, with members often working in the same space, allowing them the opportunity to build greater understanding and personal relationships. However, the case is not proven that small teams ensure creativity and large ones inhibit it. There are times when larger groups are valuable, especially when there is a need to build consensus within the organisation. The difficulty with a larger team is the potential for imbalance and increased tension, as more people become involved with different – perhaps contradictory – agendas. In addition, the larger the group, the stronger the tendency to play down personal needs in favour of team or organisational needs. This tends to demotivate people, as they feel unable to express their individuality and leads to the formation of internal tribes.

This tendency towards imbalance in larger teams often imposes the need for greater management control, which in turn reduces the potential for creativity. When organisational needs or the personal needs of senior managers are seen to dominate, people feel their input is devalued and that the potential for innovation lacks flexibility. During our research, we observed that the onset of this imbalance produced rapid results. Team members quickly began to lose trust, reduce their identification with team goals and stop contributing to sessions. This process could also be seen in smaller groups on occasion, but here it was easier to identify the problem and manage the situation.

Having observed several of the subject companies over many months, we came to realise that successful teams had a diverse personality and skill mix, yet shared values. As one manager remarked 'we are all different but the same'. What is interesting is the apparent belief that as well as sound craft skills, team members should also bring something extra in terms of personality and experience in the context of how they might complement other team members. This supports the views of many writers (for example Amabile 2001; Ford and Gioia 2000; Henry 2001a; Thompson and Brajkovich 2003) that difference, in both skill and personality mix, are key factors in generating energy, interaction and a creative climate. Without differences of knowledge, style and personality, teams can quickly develop group-think with perspectives and debate becoming confined by a static framework of understanding. This indicates the benefit of refreshing teams with new people and new inputs so that ideas keep flowing. Without diversity and its resulting tension, the creative climate can become de-energised. Similarly, it is critical to understand and balance different styles, philosophies and skills among groups in order to maximise diversity, yet minimise the potential for conflict. Without the right balance, constructive discussion and idea generation can be reduced. Too much diversity in personalities and experience may not provide a common frame of reference for the team and may increase the potential for conflict and tribalistic behaviour. Too much homogeneity can lead to inertia and a lack of creativity. Here's an example of the latter from the writer and one-time Creative Paradox at Hallmark Cards, Gordon MacKenzie. He tells the story of a task force meeting he attended where the endless presentation of statistics soon put the attendees into a stupor. Apparently this was the way the group meetings always went. As an outsider, MacKenzie subverted the process by first asking people to meditate and then to shout out everything they hated about sales meetings. After filling six pages, he asked the group to then create a new way of doing meetings. As he describes it, the group exploded with ideas. His reflection on his disruptive role was:

I think the group's initial fixation on statistical anchors – via the static medium of the overhead projector – was in step with the analysis-oriented corporate norm. In obsessing over the history represented by their statistics, the group was being *culturally* appropriate. But it was being *functionally* inappropriate, because the goal of the meeting was *supposed* to have been to create new sales meeting concepts … Release from their inculcated culture allowed the task members to metamorphise – for a little while – from mere attendants at a meeting into vibrant participants in an evolving endeavor.

(MacKenzie 1998, p206)

A networked structure

Creative teams exhibit the same essential characteristics as those of creative organisations: trust, autonomy, support and diversity. This has implications for the structuring of teams, with a move away from standard role designations and associated hierarchies to a far more networked-based model similar to Morgan's (1997) spider plant model. Although his concept is aimed at a macro level, the principle of self-organised networks supported by a mother plant and in continuous communication with other offshoots, can readily be applied at the team level. Teams need focus, support and resources. They require enough freedom to experiment, take risks and decide their own futures, but they also need to feel safe, valued and grounded in a context that they can understand and relate to. Overreliance on traditional role designations can hinder the creative process by reducing people's desire to step out of character and input a new perspective, as well as reinforcing traditional power behaviour. However, the absence of any formal allocation of responsibility can reduce focus and may prevent the development of a balanced culture, with people being afraid to experiment, take risks or champion ideas. Again there needs to be a balance. Figure 6.2, which is an extrapolation of Morgan's (1997) model shows how this can be achieved.

In this model, each team is clearly supported by the central plant and also connects with other relevant teams to ensure the cross-fertilisation of ideas. The central plant helps to set direction and provide resources. The team enjoys autonomy but does so within a

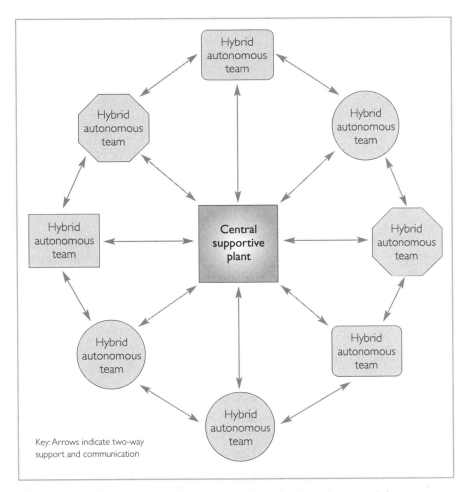

Figure 6.2 Adaptation of Morgan's hybrid spider plant model
Source: Morgan (1997, p82)

context of overall shared values. There is a regular transfer of information and feedback between the central plant and each team. This allows the centre to ensure the team is on the right strategic track and it is reassuring for the team to know that their efforts are in tune with corporate direction. However, we should recognise that the structure does not mean a 'one-size-fits-all' approach. Each team needs to be managed in the appropriate way, based on task, composition and character.

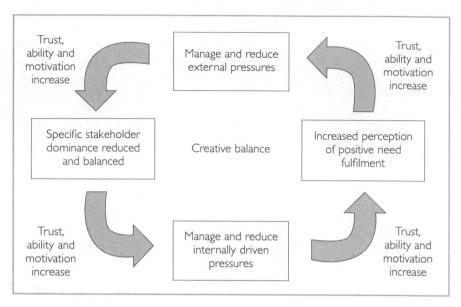

Figure 6.3 Managing for creative balance

The management of creative teams

One of the major challenges facing managers is how to balance the tensions within the team to foster a creative climate. The management model in Figure 6.3, which can be used in wider organisational environments, is also highly applicable in a team context. Managers have to deal with and balance similar external organisational and client pressures within a team context. The model details the broad forces at play and how they can be managed.

Balancing support and autonomy

The previous section highlighted the need to develop team formations similar to Morgan's (1997) model by using a self-organised network of integrated teams supported by a core organisation. This creates an effective internal environment but, as we can see in Figure 6.3, managers also need to manage the external pressures placed upon the team by clients, the organisation and other stakeholders and they need to reconcile the sometimes countervailing ideas of these different groups. To a large degree, success relies on the quality and commitment of team members, which relates back to the ability of managers to recruit staff who exhibit such characteristics. Management has to set and agree the key objectives, but needs to move away from the 'boss-director' role to the 'coach-facilitator' or 'coach-editor' role. As we will see with Volvo and Tate Modern, the coach-editor needs to define boundaries and remind people, as Simons (1995) suggests, what not to do rather than what they must do. This process is very delicate and requires a high level of skill and emotional intelligence.

The most common problem seems to be over-control, or the implementation of inflexible and too tight boundaries. This often takes the form of idea direction or decisions being made from outside the team environment. In the context of a design consultancy this sometimes leads to the designers in a team feeling they have little or no control over the direction of projects or the way in which the design process is developed. The following quote from a designer typifies the frustration:

> As we have said before, we never really get to go to meetings … The company structure does create distance between designer and client. Basically they will do exactly what the client wants and will not argue the case. Account directors and other non-designers will go and see clients and not stand up for us. The client says, 'I want this' and they say, 'OK' without involving us in anyway. It's ridiculous. Designers should be involved with the clients more and we don't get a look in at all. It's all Chinese whispers. The client tells the account director, who tells the team leader, who passes it on to senior designers and then us, finally, here. We don't know why something is being done in so many cases. Also, if we have an idea it may be passed onto the client via a third or fourth party who probably does not explain the concept properly. We do not have any feeling of ownership or involvement in a project. It is always those above us who are telling us what needs to be done.
>
> *(Personal communication)*

This situation is in stark contrast to the case studies we highlight in this book. For example, the architectural and design practice Gensler recognises that there is a conflict because the client, the project manager and the designer have different needs. However when there is a strong common culture in the organisation – or what Gensler call 'collegiality' – there is the potential for equilibrium. This is how CEO, Ed Friedrichs, describes it:

Designers by definition want to take a risk; to challenge; to stretch. Clients by definition are risk averse. So the challenge of creativity is to ameloriate risk. It's about taking a risk and then testing it enough to know it's not going to fail. Failure is unacceptable. The lawsuits are too expensive. You can't have unacceptable risk. So the issue of risk is, how do you test that risk? If you aren't confronting that risk though then you're just doing safe stuff. Achieving the balance is tremendously difficult. It's not that you ever solve the problem: there is no solution. By definition it is the act of doing it, that determines success. The project management side of the firm will always create charts and graphs and checklists and steps to make sure that risk is avoided. And designers want to tear it all up. They think it takes all the creativity out of it. So you have to keep the managers from bureaucratising design and designers from running roughshod over managers. Balancing those two things is a process of negotiation. You can stretch and test and experiment but the dialogue has to go on ... That *is* design. It's not a matter of whether it is easy or hard. It just is. Creativity comes when there is a high degree of mutual respect.

(Interview with author dated 21 August 2003)

A second common way that managers constrain their teams is the introduction of a process model that prescriptively describes how projects should be approached. In such a situation, the team can perceive its role as one of technician or supplier, rather than expert or consultant. Without any freedom to express its vision, the team may become demotivated with a consequent loss of commitment. Managers need to understand that, although process parameters are valuable as a guide to action, the team has to have enough autonomy to develop and agree detailed goals and objectives. Allowing teams the opportunity to self-organise sends a powerful signal as it communicates a high level of trust in the ability of the team. It also develops commitment, as the team feels more responsible about its future. However, self-organisation does not deny the importance of management support. Aardman Animations provides a good template for the management of creative teams. The overall management philosophy has already been illustrated. Its focus is on creating a supportive learning environment, which allows individuals the freedom to experiment within an emotionally safe context. This view appears to extend to the way in which teams are organised and managed, relying on a high degree of trust and interdependency between team members and managers.

The way this works in practice is that managers establish a degree of balance between homogeneity and heterogeneity by the use of core animation-production personnel. These animators belong to a set team of between five and eight people who form a network reporting to a director. They may work together on a number of projects at any one time, although in different combinations, allowing managers to fit skills and personalities to each project, in an attempt to build sound relationships between designers. This concept is continued as a template by the use of interdependent networks of support/account staff who similarly work with each other on a variety of projects for clients. This not only increases familiarity, but also allows managers to fit personalities and skills with projects, clients and other team members. The objective is to create a network-based team structure that balances diversity and homogeneity and that can support itself by drawing upon the skill sets available. Once the team has been chosen for a project and key objectives agreed, which involves discussion between team members and managers, senior management steps back and assumes a hands-off, monitoring role. The team is given the freedom to explore and develop the project without significant interference from senior managers. However, it is encouraged to seek advice, support or input from managers, although this is not mandatory. Senior management is involved at key internal meetings, monitoring and mentoring, but not involved in client meetings unless requested. This system appears to work for a number of reasons. First, the high degree of trust between employees results in positive perceptions and behaviour. The team can be trusted to produce quality work and communicate with management if the need arises. Second, the quality of staff is high, with key members having the skills, knowledge and experience to manage complex projects. Third, members are aware of their area of responsibility and, although encouraged to input into the whole process, remain focused. Finally, management and support staff provide a protective framework within which animators and production staff can work without significant distraction or fear.

On a closing point, it is important to note that although over-control of teams can adversely affect the creative process, too little involvement will often have a negative effect. When management fails to support staff, particularly in terms of resource allocation and conflict resolution, cross-functional teams will often break into subgroups, reducing communication and cooperation and increasing conflict.

Managing conflict and tribalism

A historical problem facing the management of creative teams is the existence of tribalism between different functional departments, and in particular the designation of people, especially in such fields as design, advertising and film, as 'creatives' and 'non-creatives'. The problem facing managers relates to a combination of embedded perceptions and differing needs that create tensions. If correctly balanced these tensions can enrich the problem-solving process; if imbalance occurs, teams often revert to stereotypical tribalistic behaviour.

The belief that 'non-creatives' create a barrier between 'creatives' and clients/customers, while making unilateral decisions, has long fostered resentment. It has already been suggested that a sense of ownership is a key motivator for creative professionals who perceive that if this is removed or diluted they will experience a loss of power and status. When the climate is negative, personal and subgroup needs unbalance creativity and generate political heat and conflict. This problem has been recognised by many writers, but few offer meaningful solutions. Our judgement is that conflict is often created when parties hold autonomous positions (often reflected in both physical and social separation) without realising the need for interdependency and the advantages of cooperation. In many of the companies we have studied, the structures, systems and management of teams created a climate of mistrust between 'creatives' and 'non-creatives'. To overcome this, managers must shift the balance back towards reciprocal interdependency, with work-flow moving equitably back and forth between parties. For this to occur managers need to communicate and emphasise the value of greater interdependency, rewarding teams that exhibit such behaviour. Ensuring that 'non-creatives' are empowered to coordinate and administer projects is important, but they should not act as a barrier between 'creatives' and clients/customers. In addition, it is important to make clear that while their input is required and valued, they are not in a situation to make unilateral decisions. Finally, facilitating communication between stakeholders is essential in helping to develop an understanding of roles, responsibilities and potential areas of conflict. This foundation of knowledge and understanding is critical to building an environment of openness and trust where conflicts can be resolved early on and relationships facilitated.

Conclusion

The pyramid shaped model presented in Figure 6.1 shows the relational tensions present in creative projects and helps to illustrate the need for managers, staff and other stakeholders to respect the balance between individual needs. Understanding which forces are creating tensions within the team dynamic, what their consequences could be in terms of perception and behaviour, and how best to manage them for balance, is a critical management task. Like creative organisations, creative teams exhibit the essential ability to balance trust, autonomy, support and diversity. It is vital that the design and management of teams focus on developing and maintaining an environment that can support and facilitate such characteristics. Balancing the needs of internal and external team stakeholders is a critical part of this process. Favouring the needs of one stakeholder over another can create an unbalanced team dynamic and reduce creativity.

Team structures should move away from traditional role designation and hierarchical forms to a far more network-based model. Traditional designs can hinder the creative process by pigeon-holing staff and reducing their desire to step out of character and input a new perspective, as well as reinforcing traditional power behaviour. However, it is important that managers do not make the mistake of creating a structure without any substantial support systems. Freedom without support will not work, as teams and the creative process need focus, structure and resources. Teams must be free enough to experiment, take risks and decide their own futures, but it is important they feel safe, valued and grounded in a context that they understand and relate to.

An important issue facing managers in this context relates to developing the correct balance between diversity and homogeneity. Balancing an organisation's personalities, skills and experiences is critical to energising the creative dynamic, as it brings a variety of perspectives to the idea generation process and helps maintain a team climate focused on debating and learning. Without such a balance teams can easily become blinkered, de-energised and de-skilled, resulting in creative stagnation. However, it is important that managers ensure there is balance between diversity and homogeneity and that individual stakeholder needs do not become dominant. If personality, skill and experience mixes are too diverse, team members will have no common frame of reference from which to establish trust-based relationships. Without this in place, it may be difficult to encourage constructive behaviour. As with organisational culture, we suggest that the answer lies in developing and maintaining the existence of fundamental core values that provide the foundation for the teams' value system. Without such a shared basis of understanding, teams run the risk of becoming fractionalised or disenfranchised, increasing the likelihood of tribalistic and creatively negative behaviour.

In addition to balancing diversity, managers are also faced with the issue of how to balance the need for autonomy against that of control. Traditional control management is a barrier to creative relationships and behaviour, as it places too much extrinsic pressure on teams and reduces environmental flexibility. Such management methods increase conflict and politically oriented behaviour, reducing levels of intrinsic motivation and trust between stakeholders. Accepting that their role needs to change is a critical requirement for managers, as is understanding that their focus can now be on supporting, protecting and nurturing teams in an attempt to build high levels of team trust, vision and motivation. Without this underlying framework, teams may find it difficult to develop the levels of positive interdependence needed to encourage experimentation and openness.

Finally, we believe that it is vital for managers to meet the needs of both organisation and client/customer, which requires them to balance creative team freedom and constraints. It appears that too many prescriptive boundaries generate an inflexible risk-averse environment. However, too few can create instability, lack of direction and fear. Managers must provide a supportive, protective, guiding and commercially oriented structure and style of management that enables self-expression and experimentation, yet ensures that the organisation is client/customer focused. It is suggested that this can best be achieved by providing clear yet flexible role and responsibility boundaries within the team, and ensuring an equitable distribution of power.

LESSONS FOR CREATIVITY

■ To deliver effective creativity, organisations need to balance the different needs of the organisation itself, the employee, the team and the customer/client

■ Managers need to provide structure, support and inspiration to the team, but the role should be one of coach-editor; the team itself should have autonomy within specified boundaries. This increases the sense of commitment and ownership

■ Successful teams have a diverse personality and skill mix, but share values; diversity is vital, because it is a spur to creativity

■ The key to getting the diversity/homogeneity balance right is emotional intelligence

7 Cultural Creativity

When the artist, Tracey Emin, exhibited her slept-in and unmade bed,[1] complete with discarded underwear, condoms, full ashtrays and empty vodka bottles the reactions were unsurprising: tabloid press disgust, a protest by two students who engaged in a pillow fight and much outraged muttering. None of this was new. From Manet's *Olympia* to Marcel Duchamp's urinal, through to Carl Andre's bricks,[2] art has regularly offended the media and the public. Indeed, since Duchamp and the emergence of conceptual art, it is no longer clear to many people exactly what art is. This creates confusion and unease, especially for the museums that sit at the nexus between the artist and the public. Yet, it is the museum that most often defines art. If Emin's bed remained in her home, it would simply be an untidy bed. By placing it in the context of a museum it becomes an insight into someone's life; the public exposure of a normally private domain. The bed and Emin become a point of discussion. We look and say: Is this art? What must her life be like? Do you think she's creative? How could she show this to people? The fact we ask these questions means something. It means success for Emin. It means provocation and engagement. It means art can be relevant and exciting. However, our concern in this book is not so much with the artist, as with the organisation. Here we can ask: What does it take to understand and manage this type of creativity? How can creativity be nurtured? How can the different needs of visitors, artists, and funders be balanced? Using the examples of Louisiana Museum of Modern Art in Denmark, Tate Modern in London,[3] Glyndebourne Opera in Sussex and Moderna Museet in Sweden, this chapter will look at the challenges of managing creativity in arts organisations.

A question of balance

Arts organisations, like businesses, have to manage countervailing forces. They have a responsibility to their audiences or visitors, but they also have a responsibility towards artists, as well as the cultural well-being of society in general; most have a responsibility to preserve the successes of the past while also confronting the future; most have to think about financial viability while taking high-profile risks. Creativity occurs by managing the tensions inherent in these paradoxes. Lars Nittve, who has managed Louisiana, Tate Modern and Moderna Museet, and David Pickard, the general manager of Glyndebourne, both believe that although their organisations' identities affect the way they manage this paradox it is possible to satisfy visitors *and* artists; to preserve *and* challenge; to be professional *and* courageous. For example, the Louisiana Museum of Modern Art, which was founded in 1958 in Humlebæk in Denmark has always had a strong focus on visitors and this is absorbed into the culture. The museum was the inspiration of Danish businessman Knud Jensen and reflected his experience of the inward-looking, institutional feel of many museums. Nittve, who was the first director of the museum after the founder says:

> The architecture, the choice of setting are designed to make you feel welcome – more like you're in somebody's home than in an institution. You enter it through the smallest building, which is a country house. You're driven round the place by your own curiosity. It was designed to prevent museum fatigue and make people open to the experience of the art. It never had uniformed guards. It was one of the first major museums with a café and a restaurant. There was an ethos – we never talked about visitors; they were always guests. That had an impact on how you thought about people and how

you related to them ... there was a strong sense of family, an informal approach and, relatively, a lack of hierarchy.

(Interview with author dated 13 November 2003)

From a visitor perspective, this sounds like plaudits. However, Nittve is critical as well, because he believes that there were periods when there was an imbalance and the focus on guests and business was overemphasised and not enough attention was paid to the art:

When I came to the museum, I felt the carriage was in front of the horses. There was a sort of feeling that you had to create a programme that would bring in the punters for the shop and the restaurant and the membership. The *raison d'être* was reversed.

(Interview with author dated 13 November 2003)

Equally the imbalance can be the other way. This is typified by some museums where the focus is all on the art and visitors are treated as a secondary issue – if they are considered much at all.

A meeting place

Getting the balance right between the audience and the art requires the idea of the organisation to be reframed as a meeting place. As Tracey Emin's *My Bed* illustrates, art is dynamic, confrontational and forever changing. It reflects people's lives, but it must also challenge them. The choice of art cannot be dictated by market research or by merely what is comfortable. Glyndebourne knows that it could sell popular operas such as *Die Fledermaus* and *Die Zauber-flöte* many times over, but equally it knows that if it only produced Strauss and Mozart it would stagnate creatively and fail to fulfil its founder's obsession of presenting, 'not the best we can do, but the best that can be done anywhere' (www.glyndebourne.com). In addition any such lack of creative courage would reduce artists' and staff's intrinsic motivation, energy and commitment to the brand which would in turn affect the quality of productions. The desire to be innovative and the goal of artistic excellence are key drivers of creativity. However, without an audience that creativity is meaningless. So, while challenging people, arts organisations also encourage access and engagement. Glyndebourne does this by touring around the UK, doing about 40 performances a year at reduced prices, by its education work and also by producing operas, such as *Tangier Tattoo*, specially created for (and with input from workshops) 18–30 year olds. At Moderna Museet in Stockholm, access has long been talked about, but it was only with the closure of the museum for two years because of a problem with mould in the building that it was realised. The crisis was a catalyst for reviewing the purpose of the museum. By default, the museum recognised that it was not its physical presence that was fundamental, but rather the collection of art and its audience. The museum took the opportunity to fulfil its mandate as the Swedish national collection of modern art, rather than that of a Stockholm museum. It invited, via the media, museums and art galleries around the country to say what they would do with the collection if they could have it. Out of the 80 responses the ten most innovative ideas were chosen. Additionally, an artmobile, comprising a large, 60-square-metre trailer was equipped as a travelling museum that visited small towns and villages. Art events were created on the internet, large-scale projections were done in the main square in Stockholm and interesting buildings were used to host contemporary exhibitions. The number of people attending Moderna Museet events doubled during this period, even without its permanent home. This closer connection to people all over Sweden impacted on the attitudes of employees. Nittve says:

> I think they're passionate about the museum and the art. And I think they're growing more passionate about the audience.
>
> *(Interview with author dated 13 November 2003)*

Nittve goes on to argue that creating an effective meeting place, where creativity works, also has implications for organisational structure. While traditional market research may be of limited value in an arts organisation, feedback is vital, especially from employees who interact directly with audiences. Without this, the organisation runs the risk of becoming deaf to the inputs of visitors. Both Nittve and Pickard agree that the ideas of employees are best heard when the organisational structure is flat. Hierarchical structures put barriers in the way of effective upwards communication and prevent genuine empowerment. Their solution has been to take layers out of the organisation, to delegate authority to people and to trust them to do the right thing. Nittve summed up this view arguing that it was vital:

> to believe in people and use less control. It's a much more Scandinavian-like management style. You work with proper delegation. Not say that you delegate and then take things back as soon as you get a bit worried.
>
> *(Interview with author dated 13 November 2003)*

Modern and contemporary

Just as Glyndebourne tries to achieve a balance between classical and more adventurous works, so Tate Modern, which opened in May 2000, has tried to balance the needs of modern and contemporary art. From the 1920s, when MOMA in New York was formed, onwards, modern art museums have tried to collect the most important works of the modern era. These collections include Picasso, Matisse, Duchamp, Warhol, Rothko, Pollock and other masters of 20th-century art. Whereas once these artists were contemporary, they are now merely modern. Mostly, while they once shocked, they are now comfortable. And while once they might have been a commercial risk, they now pull the crowds. When a Cézanne exhibition was held at the Tate in the 1990s it drew over 400,000 people. Contemporary art is different. It may be uncomfortable, its quality is more difficult to evaluate and public interest is uncertain. Yet contemporary art is an important element for a modern museum, partly because the 'modern' works of tomorrow are contained in the contemporary, but also because contemporary work creates excitement and dialogue and challenges ideas about creativity. Many modern art museums have tended to concentrate on the modern. With Tate Modern, Nittve consciously tried to create a balance by developing a structure that could do big, well-researched, serious exhibitions and also do small, fast-moving, contemporary shows. This had implications for both recruitment and leadership.

To help ensure that both modern and contemporary strands co-existed and that creative ideas would cover both areas, Tate Modern and Glyndebourne consciously recruit key people who have breadth and depth of experience in both major and smaller institutions. Individuals who have the intellectual ability and the nous to work on long-term projects, but who also have the energy, initiative and confidence to take decisions and make them work. As Nittve argues:

> To take a decision in the morning and do something about it in the afternoon, not the following year.
>
> *(Interview with author dated 13 November 2003)*

Having recruited such people, both Nittve and Pickard have tried to create an open, communicative and informal structure, where they could express their ideas and operate with minimal interference. This was important both for an individual sense of fulfilment, but also for the smooth operation of teams. The role of the leader in this case was to define a sense of direction and then to inspire and support individuals. Nittve believes that this helped Tate Modern to generate a high-trust culture and a highly creative environment:

> I can't think of any areas where there is a need for creativity where it can work without a high level of trust. Trust in the sense that if someone is given responsibility, they're trusted to take that and run with it. But also you need to create a climate that is a safe place for ideas and where you can say stupid things, but you're not made to look stupid. It's about trying to create a non-blame culture … on the other hand people need to be responsible. That's a difficult balance.
>
> *(Interview with author dated 13 November 2003)*

The power of money

All art organisations strive for excellence, but are constrained by financial necessity. Glyndebourne has no subsidy (a rarity in the world of government-subsidised opera) which means it has to charge high ticket prices and needs to balance the more experimental with the safe. Pickard, says, 'it means we have to have a commercial edge which sometimes counteracts our creative aspirations'. However, the £8 million generated from their summer season helps fund the more unusual, modern and creative work produced for their tours. Even so, there can be too much originality, as in 2002 when Glyndebourne pushed too far and suffered at the box office. As a result Pickard recognises that in future years a better balance between commercial and creative needs will need to be achieved:

It's right to tilt the balance a bit that way, but once people ask, 'what's so special about this?' you have a big problem. Then you damage their trust.

(Interview with author dated 9 September 2003)

Similarly, when the Tate organisation came under financial pressure, Tate Modern had to change the modern/contemporary balance in favour of the modern. Nittve feels that change was a loss:

It works absolutely fine for the wider audience, but I think you lose the connections into the art world and particularly the London art world.

(Interview with author dated 13 November 2003)

The implication is that the idea of balance between the different responsibilities of an arts organisation is an ideal. There will be internal cultural pressures and funding constraints that upset the equilibrium and, as a result, inhibit creativity. There are also pressures on the creative balance we saw in Chapter 6, where the inter-relationship between personal, team, organisational and client needs has to be managed. However, the desire and vision to be creative sustains corporate energy and creative drive.

A real work of art

The arts are much concerned with the nature of reality. Either the artifice of art is exposed, as in Magritte's painting that features a pipe with the exhortation *Ceci n'est pas une pipe,* or reality is affirmed as in Mark Wallinger's, *A Real Work of Art,* which was actually a horse that the artist bought and raced in the 1994 flat-racing season. To achieve creative balance, organisations have to confront this issue of reality. Managers can either accept the abstraction and artifice of existing organisational structures and processes or they can think anew about the reality of the way people truly think, behave, interact and generate new ideas. Tate Modern is a powerful example of this approach, because as a new organisation it provided the opportunity to rethink the relationships internally among employees and also externally with visitors. This led, among other things, to a different approach to curating.

Generally the curation of modern art is done chronologically. However, Nittve and his curatorial team decided to adopt a thematic approach. Partly this was a practical issue. The interest in modern art among directors of the Tate had wavered over the years, which resulted in a strong, but uneven, collection. It was felt that a chronological presentation would only emphasise the gaps. Partly the decision was based on some views about modern art and the way people viewed it. Three elements were important here. First, whereas history has traditionally tended to be viewed as a search for objective truth, increasingly people have come to recognise that it is subjective; the perspective of the historian or writer taints it. As the historian of ideas, Michel Foucault (1991a, p88) says, 'knowledge is not made for understanding, it is made for cutting'. In other words, there is not one institutional truth, but many truths. Second, as modern art so aptly demonstrates, it is difficult to always be certain. The principle of uncertainty suggests there are different ways of interpreting ideas and seeing things – as Tate Modern says in its curatorial statement about cubism: 'solid apprehensible reality seems to give way to a world of shifting relationships.' Third, as the new media thinker Douglas Rushkoff (2001), suggests, people need to have shorter, multiple stories if their interest is to be maintained.[4] The result of these different strands of thinking led to the development of four distinct curatorial themes:

1. History/Memory/Society

2. Landscape/Matter/Environment

3. Nude/Action/Body

4. Still Life/Object/Real Life.

Within each theme there were also subthemes and interesting, thought-provoking juxtapositions, such as within the Landscape theme, there is a subtheme of Geometry of Nature. Here we find a multi-coloured, paper-cut-out swirl by Matisse from 1953, which was originally called *The Snail*, but was subsequently renamed *Chromatic Composition*, next to Ellsworth Kelly's[5] 1974 *White Curve*, which uses shape and colour to suggest landscape. Interspersed is a Calder mobile with its tree-like balance and movement. The viewer is not just invited to view the works of art, but is located within a landscape that inspires associations and ideas about other landscapes.

The process of determining the thematic approach and then executing it was collective and expresses some of our core themes in this book, especially in terms of freedom and structure. The definition of the thematic approach was the result of a small and cohesive core team of Lars Nittve, two curators and an education curator, who worked to the key principles they had defined. However to avoid group-think, the group was then expanded into a think tank with artists, philosophers and art historians. Nittve says about this diversity:

> I think we valued different voices and we also knew that we all came from the same direction. And it's not given that that is the only direction. At certain moments in processes it's good to have some friction, because it breaks up patterns and models of thinking. Sometimes you're moving too automatically … also we wanted to move towards having different voices in how we displayed and talked about the collection; to move away from this institutional voice to a more multiple voice.
>
> *(Interview with author dated 13 November 2003)*

At this stage the boundaries of creativity were defined by the vision for Tate Modern, but within those boundaries there was considerable latitude. Once the four themes had been realised through this interaction, the requirements changed. The goal now was to flesh out the basic themes and to test the viability of ideas. Whereas the first group required diversity of background, the new groups, who would explore the themes, needed to have diversity of knowledge but within a cohesive field. A series of bigger think tanks was formed with curators from the Tate's central collection. These people used their specific expertise to define how the four themes could be realised from the works that the Tate owned. Finally, once the bigger think tanks had reached agreement, a small group was formed to fine tune and detail each individual room within the themes. This tighter group was less about diversity and more about unity. Nittve, says of the last group:

> When you install the collection it has to have a similar tone of voice. It's enough that you get very different positions and statements in the works of art, because you have very different artists. If the mode of installation and presentation is very

different from room to room it might just turn chaotic. That's why we had a
smaller team under one person who was responsible for bringing that together.
(Interview with author dated 13 November 2003)

This 'accordion-like' process within Tate Modern was designed
to adapt to the requirements of creativity – providing different
levels of diversity and homogeneity at different times. At the earlier
stage, when the creative boundaries were at their broadest, diversity was encouraged to help create connections that might not have
been seen by a narrowly defined group. However, when the level of
creativity in the later stages became more detailed and the boundaries were narrow, homogeneity was more valuable. At this point,
the requirement was not to question the fundamental approach to
curating the museum, but rather to provide creativity in the
specifics of installation.

Leading teams and respect

We might read the description of the teams at Tate Modern above
and wonder how one can know when to have a small group or a
large one; when to have a diverse group and when to have a cohesive
one. Of course, there is no tick box method for always getting this
right, although some of the ideas outlined in the previous chapter
give an indication of what to do when. The truth is that structuring
groups requires respect, clarity of vision, sensitivity and trust.

Respect

Whether respect goes with a title or has to be earned varies within
cultures. Lars Nittve found that in the UK, the title of Director confers
authority, whereas in Sweden, respect has to be earned. Swedish
culture encourages the questioning of authority and the idea that no
one is better than anyone else. Within arts organisations, respect also
requires an in-depth knowledge of the art form. Nittve's long experience of teaching, writing and curating helped substantiate his position.
Equally, David Pickard at Glyndebourne finds that his musical education provides him with credibility in managing performers. When this

credibility doesn't exist it creates a lack of confidence and trust. Not only does David Pickard have respect for artists and performers, he is equally admiring of all members of staff from gardeners and drivers to sound engineers and scene painters. Of particular importance is his respect for his senior directors:

> I really respect what they [his directors] say and I would be very reluctant to do something they disagreed with. It has always been important for me to have a strong team around me, so my role is to lead and make decisions but informed from people around me who have greater knowledge about each area than I do.
>
> *(Interview with author dated 13 November 2003)*

Clarity of vision

Both Pickard and Nittve stress the importance of being honest and open. To create effective groups, the goals and the constraints need to be clearly defined and communicated at the outset. This cannot be a cosmetic exercise. The reason for involving others is to make full use of the intellectual capital you have at your disposal, but people need to know why they have been selected, what the requirements are and how success will be judged. It is equally important that the brand vision is clear, so it can act as a creative beacon and focusing tool. Pickard stresses the value of Glyndebourne's unique heritage as a force that guides and moulds the organisation's actions:

> I think a lot of the closely knit feeling here comes from its [Glyndebourne] astonishing history ... when you are sticking labels on wine bottles you kind of feel you are part of that crazy vision of 1934 when John Christie built a theatre for his wife to sing in. That slight eccentricity he had is part of this place, and drives us to strive for excellence. He had this phrase 'our aim here is not to do the best we can but the best that can be done anywhere' and we trot it out again and again. It is very powerful, people remember and understand where we want to go.
>
> *(Interview with author dated 9 September 2003)*

Sensitivity

Picking the right people to take part in a group, judging the size and knowing when to change or close down the group requires leaders who are capable of managing both individual and organisational needs. To do this well requires an in-depth understanding of individual technical skills and personality traits and the ability to inspire people to make full use of their talents. Additionally, if the culture is informal, it is possible to bring in people from outside the group. Nittve says about the Moderna Museet:

> We work in a very team-oriented way. I really do believe when we develop ideas, it should not only be the group that develops ideas. It's good to bring in others who are surprised to bring in their ideas. Often they can be the ones who are the catalysts.
>
> *(Interview with author dated 13 November 2003)*

Trust

Pickard and Nittve recognise that they do not have all the answers. In fact they embrace this realisation, understanding that creativity is a socially dynamic process that relies on variety of knowledge, cooperation and positive interaction between a number of people. Having the courage to accept this concept is a crucial step, enacting it requires intelligence and trust. As leaders, both are able to step back from their teams, giving them free rein to explore, debate possibilities and act creatively, because they trust their staff to act in a professional and honest manner. They trust their teams' intentions, skills and abilities and are able to act in a far more editorial role, filtering, refining and focusing ideas. Trust is two-way and must be earned, but without it managers and teams cannot hope to act creatively.

Conclusion

Woody Allen's (1975) description of his ambition to 'forge in the smithy of my soul the uncreated conscience of my race. And then see if I can get them mass-produced in plastic' is an ironic summary of the challenge for art organisations. On the one hand artistic integrity and cultural relevance needs to be maintained. On the other, funding is a constant potential compromiser. Lars Nittve argues that these pressures ought not to be irreconcilable; arts organisations should be both/and. The arts should be both challenging and accessible. This tension between the two polarities should be the spur for creativity. This is best realised through the effective use of groups, bringing together the necessary specific knowledge and diverse viewpoints. The role of the leader here is to set direction and to coach individuals. We might ask whether this approach to creativity works. In performance terms it seems to. Glyndebourne is a rarity as a long-established, commercially successful, non-subsidised opera organisation with a powerful brand; Moderna Museet has doubled its audience, increased access and discarded entrance fees and Tate Modern received critical plaudits when it opened and 4.6 million visitors in the first ten months (against a projected target of 2.5 million for the first year).

LESSONS FOR CREATIVITY

- Non-bureaucratic self-organised and self-responsible structures help stimulate creativity

- Employees need to be genuinely empowered to make the most of their creative input

- Creativity is facilitated when the tensions and needs between countervailing forces are recognised, managed and balanced

- Teams need to have vision clarity as well as clear points of accountability and responsibility

- Teams need to understand and believe in the organisation's brand if they are to be focused, flexible and motivated

- Diversity of knowledge, experience and personality are key but must be underpinned by a set of homogenous core values that bind and focus

Notes

1 Charles Saatchi acquired *My Bed* for £150,000. It was short-listed for the 1999 Turner Prize. Although a real bed was a novelty as an artwork, beds are a common feature of art, notably in the work of French artist, Sophie Calle.

2 Manet's *Olympia* was slated by critics and became a *succès du scandale*, Marcel Duchamp's *Fountain* was rejected as indecent in 1917 by the Society of Independent Artists, while the Tate Gallery's acquisition of Carl Andre's 120 bricks laid out in a rectangular shape, *Equivalent VIII*, was mocked by the media. The *Daily Mirror* headline, 'What a load of rubbish' typified the view.

3 When Tate Modern opened in 2000, it was the first new European modern art museum since the Centre Pompidou in Paris in 1977.

4 Rushkoff has demonstrated this through his analysis of narrative in *The Simpsons*. To sustain the viewer's interest, narrative in *The Simpsons*, contains a succession of small stories.

5 Ellsworth Kelly's work shows how Matisse's insights were extended after his own lifetime.

8 Customers, Creativity and Risk

During the 1990s, successive British governments were preoccupied with the goodwill potential of a celebration of the future. Echoing the 1951 Festival of Britain: A tonic to the nation, the Millennium Dome in South London was a £750 million statement of visionary confidence. However, on hand to record the negotiations, briefings, presentations, politics, construction and general lack of vision was a television documentary team. The 4-hour BBC series – *The Dome: Trouble at the Big Top* – which began transmission just before the millennium in December 1999, was a lesson in how not to manage creativity and new product development. One of the programmes featured the development of design ideas by two consultancies, Park Avenue Productions and Land Design Studio. Park Avenue had responsibility for designing a zone within the Dome exhibition called Work and Learn, while Land Design was responsible for the Play zone. What became clear in the course of the programme was that there was a lack of clear direction, no real briefing, low confidence and trust and unclear accountability. For example, after several months of design work on a unified zone, Park Avenue discovered that there would in fact be two zones: a Work zone sponsored by Manpower and a Learn zone sponsored by Tesco. Park Avenue's response was to create a ride, even though the Dome company, the

NMEC, specifically wanted to avoid theme-park-style rides. After one year of design work, Ben Evans, zone editor of Work and Learn, described the process as 'tortuous'. Park Avenue then developed a cinematic idea, which left Evans even more frustrated:

> They [Park Avenue] haven't really been able to address our concerns on an intellectual basis, on a creative basis or on a design basis. In all of those three key areas they've been weak ... we do need to go back to the brief ... we just go round in circles. We're back to where we were.
>
> *(The Dome: Trouble at the Big Top, Part 2, BBC)*

The NMEC relationship with Land Design was equally frustrating. The sponsor for the Play zone was Sky, which wanted to feature its Sky Digital service. In this instance there was a clear conflict between the goals of the NMEC and the commercial desires of Sky. Land Design was obviously finding it hard to meet these two opposing needs, especially when they hadn't had direct contact with Sky. After having their work rejected in a condemnatory way by the NMEC reference group, one of the Land Design partners confessed that they didn't understand the brief. Sky, equally frustrated, dropped the sponsorship of the zone. None of the organisations comes across well, which makes for good and entertaining television, but the viewer is left wondering why some basic questions are never asked, such as: What is the brief? What are the goals? How will decisions be made and by whom? What is the accountability? In a creative rush to design something – anything – nobody seems to want to expend the intellectual energy at the outset to think about what might be relevant to visitors, to really analyse a brief and to think through the implications. Neither does anyone seem to invest the time to work together to build confidence and trust and to manage the interests of different audiences.

Do new ideas matter?

This chapter is concerned with how best to develop new products, services and brands. Our premise is that this is fundamentally about how to build effective creative and valuable partnerships between a managing or commissioning client and an internal team or external consultancy. These are partnerships that focus on the needs of customers and are sufficiently resourceful to implement their ideas – possibly against a backdrop of an indifferent organisation. This requires commitment and ingenuity – attributes that can be seen live in the accompanying case stories. We are, of course, making one dangerous assumption here: that new ideas do matter to organisations. We believe they should, because speed of change in the competitive environment dictates that. However, there are also some opposing forces. More than thirty years ago, Stephen King (1973), the director of research at advertising agency J. Walter Thompson wrote a small, but informative book about developing new brands. He noted that while senior managers often say that new products are the lifeblood of their organisation, in reality they abhor the upset to routine, the risk and the potential for failure.

> So development work is allowed to drift on, but the funds voted to it are kept under strict control; nobody acts as if new products were the life-blood of the company. What usually emerges from this is a fairly large number of not terribly expensive new projects, most of which fail and the best of which are only moderate profit-earners. *(p1)*

With this attitude to new product development, no one takes new ideas too seriously and no one invests too much effort in building trusting relationships. It's difficult to know how widespread this perspective is, but the lack of commitment to innovation leads to cynicism and a tendency on the part of the commissioning client to use what might be called the buyer–supplier model. This is a straightforward exchange process where the buyer buys creativity from the team. The buyer is in control and the team is subservient. This limits risks and the value creativity can add. It also tends to encourage a cursory attitude to understanding end consumers. Here teams might be informed by some focus groups and quantitative data, but there tends to be a lack of true consumer knowledge, connection and engagement. This leads to a situation whereby organisations generate new products, services and brands that exhibit little real difference in terms of benefits and value, relying instead on marketing to create a point of difference. Rightly consumers become more cynical and demanding, questioning the dream and looking for the reality of clear new benefits. These failings are why the writer Alan Mitchell (2003) says:

Instead of fulfilling their role as the consumer's friend, as trusted beacons of superior value, brands are widely perceived as superficial, exploitative, manipulative and even dehumanizing. *(p38)*

Not surprisingly, we're not very supportive of this model. We do believe in the importance of new and genuine ideas and we do believe that new ideas will only work with commitment. The examples of creative organisations in this book demonstrate that it is essential to listen and to build strong emotional, trusting partnerships with clients and customers.

Building creative partnerships

Understanding roles and needs

While NMEC is an extreme (and very public) example of an organisation that failed to build creative partnerships with others, in fact many organisations maintain structures and systems that do not really support projects, people and relationships. This leads to inhibited creativity. All those involved in new product development (NPD) have to understand each other's needs and roles within the context of the creative process. The first step should be to define and agree roles, needs and objectives for the project so helping to develop a clear, shared vision. This should be a rigorous process and a collaborative one. The client should play a pivotal role in the creative process in providing the problem, setting budgets, imposing deadlines and commercial objectives, and acting as the final decision-maker, but the innovation team needs to share in a deep understanding of the objectives. Without such involvement the innovation team runs the risk of generating ideas outside the parameters of the client's brief, or, alternatively, of trying to second-guess what the client will buy. Not only can this waste time and frustrate team members, it might also reduce the level of trust between parties, increase the likelihood of conflict and compound negatively embedded perceptions. The result of this in the case of NMEC and Park Avenue Productions was the removal of the designers from the Work and Learn zone. After more than a year of zigzagging work, the head of Park Avenue declared himself to be 'disappointed' and 'frustrated', especially as he felt, seemingly without irony, that 'the trust was starting to be there'.

The mismatch of expectations sometimes occurs because teams become complacent about their clients, believing that they know and understand their needs and aspirations. Important questions are not asked. Assumptions are made. People forget that trust has to be earned. Familiarity (or arrogance) lulls parties into a false sense of security and reduces their ability to identify and deal with potential problems early on in the relationship. Similarly, previous experience with similar companies or people can induce myopia. Rather than trying to think through a problem afresh, the temptation is to dust something off from the shelf and then try and squeeze it into a shape that matches the brief (sort of). Yet every challenge is different: the Millennium Dome was not Disney World. Each client has individual needs and expectations and resources and time should be given to understanding these and developing a shared understanding of roles, responsibilities and needs. This does not undermine the importance of operational efficiency in creative management: clear and accurate project documents, briefs and feedback systems. What it does suggest is the value of working hard to develop productive relationships. Whether such a strategy involves joint learning sessions, corporate entertaining or more straightforward social engagement, the premise is to get to know the people.

The benefits of a partnership approach are numerous. Knowledge of the client's business reduces perceived risks. In addition, understanding the client's profile helps managers to match personalities and experience to need and indicates how to manage the customer–team relationship. It increases the potential for client involvement with the project, which in turn decreases actual risk while increasing organisational buy-in. Finally, as both parties become more confident, the desire for original thinking increases as does the will to see a project through to a successful completion. Here people start to believe that new ideas are the lifeblood of the organisation.

From supplier to consultant

A major problem for many NPD and what we call new brand development (NBD) teams is the way in which they are perceived in business-to-business relationships and the impact this has on their ability or willingness to take risks and generate creative solutions.[1] As this section suggests, stakeholders should seek to achieve balance and equitable relationships. The main problem of the supplier–buyer model is the tendency for the client to dominate the situation, leading to imbalance and negative feelings on the part of the development team. The potential for clients to dictate the direction and style of creativity increases as they seek to control the process. The danger is that the development team defaults to the delivery of a safe and uncompelling solution. Within such a context, the potential for risk taking and experimentation is often reduced as relationships are defined by contractual obligation. The project climate may degenerate such that control, formalisation and the use of extrinsic motivators are dominant. As a result, the levels of commitment and cooperation exhibited by the team will be strictly limited.

The benefit of greater equality is that teams can build deeper relationships with clients, so increasing understanding and trust and allowing them fuller and early access to clients and information. As a result the creative team has the time to investigate and experiment with ideas, allowing it to find creative direction often before being constrained by deadlines or inflexible project requirements. In this context, relational tensions can be more equitable, with no single stakeholder dominating another, thus facilitating creative balance. The sense that many innovators have of not being valued as highly as other professionals has generated a tendency to resentment, which, if not managed, can reduce the potential for trusting relationships. In the worst situations, lack of client trust leads to disengagement and the production of passive variants of tried and tested solutions, rather than fresh thinking. Even though the relationship between creative team and client tends to be an unequal one, as it is the latter who holds the budget, the relationship should not be subservient. Senior managers of external consultants or internal creative teams must actively engage and not shy away from conflict if higher levels of trust, respect and equality are to be won. The need is to establish a dialogue with clients over working practices, team dynamics, protocols and project boundaries as well as needs, aspirations and expectations. This again brings us back to the issue of emotional intelligence. Managers on both sides need to overcome often stereotypical views of each other. There needs to be balance and mutual respect, not unfettered prejudice:

■ First, clients cannot always be expected to have the creative ability or vision to generate original product or brand solutions. Creative professionals are employed precisely to deliver these solutions.

■ Second, clients cannot expect full and considered solutions if information and knowledge are not properly shared. Creative professionals should know how to think creatively, but they are unlikely to know the business issues to the same degree as the client.

■ Third, there is an issue of attitude. The quality of debate and communication will be reduced if clients maintain an autocratic position or if an innovative company or team remains passive or acts in a subordinate manner. We would argue that if creative teams are held in low professional esteem, clients will be reluctant to accept advice, invest in experimentation and take creative risks.

■ Finally, if creative team managers act in a subordinate or passive manner, they run the risk of alienating their own employees, who will see the relationship as skewed in favour of the clients and undermining of their integrity.

Opening up

Emotional intelligence and the relationship between client and creative team are enhanced through involvement. Rather than either party trying to guess the motivations and fears of the other, there should be a unity of interest. Traditionally this has been inhibited by the reluctance of creative teams to include 'outsiders' preferring to keep ownership of projects and ideas to themselves, until that 'hey presto' moment when all is revealed. This has to change. Any consultancy or professional relationship requires a far more open and equal exchange of information than a traditional buyer–supplier one. Such a situation cannot be one-way: teams need to become more open and accepting of outside input, welcoming it as a way of building commitment and increasing the diversity of perspectives available to inform a project. In addition, greater client involvement increases the potential for buy-in and helps prevent misalignment of expectations evident in so many failed projects. When innovators are willing to engage with clients without fear and favour, creative possibilities are increased. This may be attributed to two factors:

1. The level of trust between stakeholders rises, reducing the potential for one stakeholder to dominate another.

2. As trust develops, benevolent behaviour, and, in particular, free information flow and dialogue, become embedded in the relationship, increasing the potential for creative idea generation and risk taking. Remember, creativity is enhanced through diverse knowledge and open debate. It is better to work together to tease out subtleties, nuances and possibilities.

Recognising that clients can be creative is a first step in building productive relationships. This leads to an openness that bears fruit in the form of high levels of trust and balance in the creative dynamic.

This also suggests that both innovators and clients need to shift their perceptions of relationships from projects to strategy: to an awareness of the long-term business benefits of innovation. Not only does this help improve the range, originality and potential value of ideas generated, it also acts as a motivational force for innovators and clients. When the perception of importance and involvement is high, there is more willingness to experiment and adopt ideas with flair. Keeping clients at a distance can only limit the knowledge available to innovators. This in turn constrains creative thinking and compounds the negative perceptions of creativity and creative people.

The ideal relationship is featured in Figure 8.1. This reaffirms the importance of putting the building blocks of creativity in place, before thinking about being creative. Most important among these is the development of a clear brief that defines a picture of the end customer, sets out a clear framework, determines accountability and inspires rather than constrains creative potential. This allows the client and the creative team to have a more equitable partnership where ideas are developed together and communication is frank and open. This is far preferable to the supplier–buyer model, where the client believes they know the solution and really only requires a

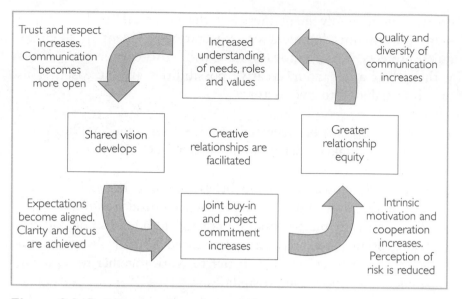

Figure 8.1 Building creative relationships

willing executioner. Team commitment shrinks to that required by contractual obligation. The result is unoriginal and safe solutions that are ultimately disappointing for both sides.

The value of process and structure

A client-focused framework

> Most brand failures start not with a failure to communicate with customers, but with failures of communication inside organizations and between organizations and consultants ... what they need is much more honest conversations with each other, and with all stakeholders. There should be fewer promises made and a greater willingness to challenge and be challenged.
>
> *(Moore 2003)*

There is always a tendency within creative teams towards narcissism. The needs of clients can become secondary to those of individuals or the team: forgotten, ignored or simply misunderstood. This reduces the potential for value creation and increases the likelihood of conflict. Clients become reluctant to take risks or delegate authority to the creative team. The way out of this negative spiral is to develop supportive client-focused structures that reinforce commitment and deliver stronger relationships. In so doing, managers must ensure that they do not alienate creative team members or inhibit open communication between the team and client. The implication, as the examples of Aardman, Gensler and others demonstrate, is that a creative team should have the support of professional people who can manage projects, budgets and deadlines properly, represent the client perspective and provide a stimulating environment for allowing creative individuals to experiment and explore ideas. However, it is important that they remain flexible and do not stray into making unilateral creative decisions. Nor should they be the sole conduit of information between creative individuals and clients as this can lead to internal conflict and misalignment of expectations. When structures relegate innovators to a subordinate role it creates disengagement and frustration. Our own experience has shown that overassertive support/account staff tend to encourage degeneration in internal relationships. This then spills over into customer relationships, eroding trust and understanding, and increasing perceptions of risk. In these circumstances, actors often revert to stereotypical supplier–buyer behaviour.

However, without good business or project management, the potential for creativity will be significantly reduced. Without supporting structures and processes, creative members can quickly lose sight of time scales, budgets and customer objectives or needs. As many have told us, they have neither the interest nor skills needed to manage the administrative or 'hard' side of the business. In addition, they may not have the business knowledge or interpersonal skills to build and maintain effective relationships with clients on their own. This creates a difficult situation for creative teams and one that requires high levels of skill to resolve, if creative balance is to be achieved. The main advantage enjoyed by the organisations we have studied stems from the recognition that innovators need to interact with clients as well as with their support staff and leaders. Client access is important for innovation teams in terms of communication, relationship development and motivation. It is equally valuable for clients. As NPD and NBD are inherently risky, clients often feel reassured and 'in control' if they are closely connected to a project.

The companies in this book ensure that all channels of communication are open and creative team members attend client meetings. In addition, a proactive effort is made to involve clients in internal meetings and idea generation sessions. The argument is that both innovators and support staff have important roles to play in the creative process. Support staff should not be excluded from idea generation or discouraged from debating ideas. The ideal role is to provide a support system that protects the interests of clients and creative team members.

Information capture and communication

As well as promoting a culture that is client-facing, it is important for organisations to make improvements in their information-capture and dissemination processes. This has for a long time been a problem area for companies trying to innovate. Inaccurate or inadequate communication leads to misalignment of expectations and a lack of focus in terms of outcomes, roles and responsibilities. Problems of this kind undermine client confidence and encourage autocratic behaviour as the perception of risk increases and the level of trust declines. It is important to address this issue. The first area to focus on is the briefing process, which involves reaching agreement on project objectives, parameters and potential creative direction. Few organisations have a process for gathering the relevant information accurately in a standard format that provides deep and rich understanding of needs, objectives and expectations. Companies typically vary their process from project to project, taking an ad hoc approach to information capture. Good information and communication is of real value in facilitating debate. It is often the case that clients are unsure of what new directions products could take or where potential innovation opportunities lie. A sound process can raise questions, highlight discrepancies in customer expectations, and help in generating a compelling creative brief. There are some examples of this cited in Chapter 11 in the approaches to briefing for the Volvo Cross Country and the VW Beetle. In both these cases it was the attention paid to the brief that provided the inspiration for the teams and ensured that all the important salient facts, requirements and customer aspirations were addressed.

Aligning expectations

A further issue that creative teams must address, especially if they are external, is how they communicate their intentions, objectives, processes, outcomes, roles and responsibilities. As with the briefing process, lack of attention in relating such details has resulted in the breakdown of many relationships. It is essential that companies clearly outline these elements for two reasons:

1. It helps ensure expectations between stakeholders are aligned.

2. It helps build trust with the client by confirming the understanding of needs and expectations.

A good example of a consultancy that thinks about these details of alignment is the branding and design company, Marketplace Design. This company specialises in the retail sector for such clients as Audi, Porsche and Elizabeth Arden. They have developed a powerful client communication tool in the form of project documentation that clearly specifies working methods, objectives and the roles and responsibilities of team members. Although such a document might be perceived by some as constraining the creative process, it provides a supportive framework for both designers and client. There is no evidence that the document has limited creativity. In fact it is seen to promote focused idea generation and innovation. Further, it provides a supportive framework that sets out the fundamentals of the project in terms of scope, boundaries, goals and objectives. By involving each of the stakeholders it prevents one group or another from becoming dominant. As with the management of account or support staff, the key lies in balancing creative tensions while lending direction, clarification and support.

Increasing trust

Figure 8.2 illustrates how a structured, client-focused framework can strengthen relationships. Without such a framework the needs of the client can become secondary to those of others, unbalancing the

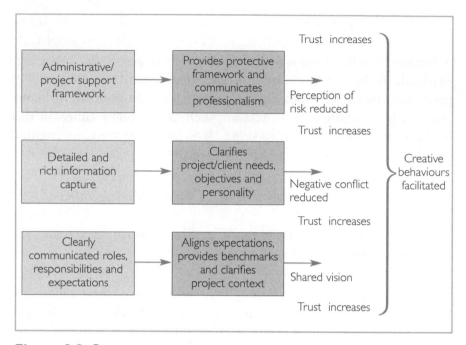

Figure 8.2 Process, structure and creative relationships

creative dynamic and increasing the potential for conflict. To ensure that the client remains at the forefront, creative teams should eschew the traditional ad hoc approach taken to client relationship management. Developing a supportive and genuinely client-focused structure can help creative organisations and teams to present a more professional image and increase trust in their reliability. This should not be intimidating to creative individuals. The word 'structure' does not automatically imply bureaucracy or over-weaning control. It should ensure creativity takes place within a business-focused process and it should ensure that the importance of communication and participation is heightened.

The corollary of this is that creative organisations should target improving the capture of information and sharing it with team members. Traditionally, poor management of this process has been a source of problems with clients and has damaged innovation. Inaccurate recording and communication of NPD/NBD briefs, customer aspirations and needs as well as a misalignment of expectations and lack of focus are all chronic problems that occur as a result. The consequence is the erosion of confidence. The information gathering process can be enhanced through the use of technology to improve data capture and facilitate improved understanding through the development of online knowledge sharing centres and innovation decision systems, such as in Figure 8.3. However, the most important strategy is to develop far closer relationships with customers enabling greater natural input and understanding to occur, resulting in information that is rich and relevant rather than sparse and limited solely to marketing statistics. In parallel, creative brands can improve the systems they use to communicate to customers their intentions, objectives, processes, outcomes, roles and responsibilities.

Conclusion

The quality and type of relationship that exists between innovation team and client is central to the creative dynamic. If trust-based, equitable partnerships are not developed, creativity can be hindered through defensive, aggressive or passive behaviour. Risk-averse attitudes, resulting from fear, mistrust and misunderstanding, lead to a reduction of intrinsic motivation and cooperation, so damaging the quality of creative relationships and debate. It is critical that customer needs and team needs become more evenly balanced than they frequently appear to be. If clients maintain their dominant position, acting in accordance with a buyer–supplier frame of reference, it is likely that the creative dynamic will remain unbalanced, reinforcing negative behaviour. In such an environment, trust-based relationships and benevolent behaviour are hard to cultivate.

Equally if clients needs are ignored, creative teams run the risk of generating ideas based on personal desire rather than business benefits. This is about the appropriate use of information. Data and knowledge can be applied prescriptively or can be used in a creative way to set up interesting and thought-provoking challenges. When this is done well, creative team members are focused and energised and clients can be more confident in the relevance of the solutions. It is the opposite of the downward spiral that could be seen in the relationship between the NMEC and its consultancies where ironically 'work' never seemed to connect with 'learn'.

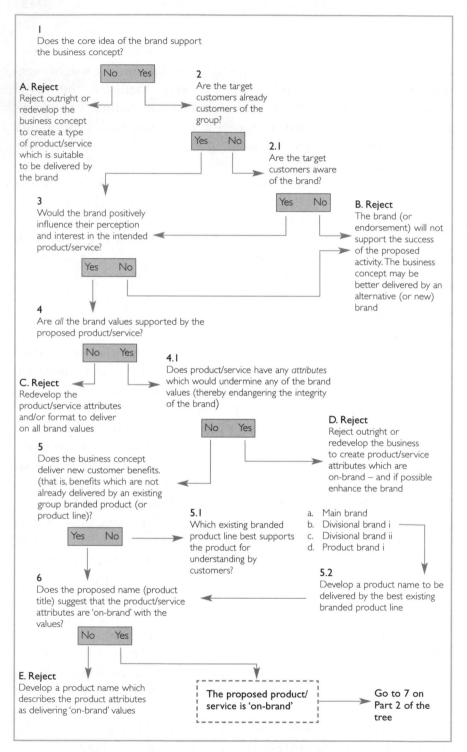

1
Does the core idea of the brand support the business concept?

No Yes

A. Reject
Reject outright or redevelop the business concept to create a type of product/service which is suitable to be delivered by the brand

2
Are the target customers already customers of the group?

Yes No

2.1
Are the target customers aware of the brand?

Yes No

B. Reject
The brand (or endorsement) will not support the success of the proposed activity. The business concept may be better delivered by an alternative (or new) brand

3
Would the brand positively influence their perception and interest in the intended product/service?

Yes No

4
Are *all* the brand values supported by the proposed product/service?

No Yes

C. Reject
Redevelop the product/service attributes and/or format to deliver on all brand values

4.1
Does product/service have any *attributes* which would undermine any of the brand values (thereby endangering the integrity of the brand)

No Yes

D. Reject
Reject outright or redevelop the business to create product/service attributes which are on-brand – and if possible enhance the brand

5
Does the business concept deliver new customer benefits. (that is, benefits which are not already delivered by an existing group branded product (or product line)?

Yes No

5.1
Which existing branded product line best supports the product for understanding by customers?

a. Main brand
b. Divisional brand i
c. Divisional brand ii
d. Product brand i

5.2
Develop a product name to be delivered by the best existing branded product line

6
Does the proposed name (product title) suggest that the product/service attributes are 'on-brand' with the values?

No Yes

E. Reject
Develop a product name which describes the product attributes as delivering 'on-brand' values

The proposed product/service is 'on-brand'

Go to 7 on Part 2 of the tree

Figure 8.3 The brand innovator's decision tree: Part I

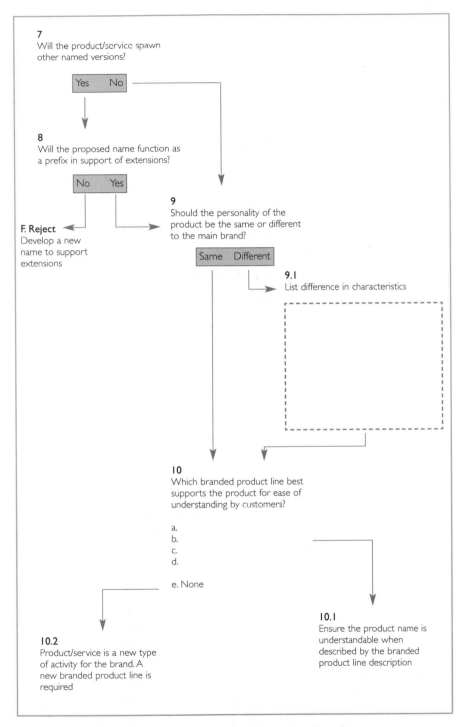

7
Will the product/service spawn
other named versions?

Yes   No

8
Will the proposed name function as
a prefix in support of extensions?

No   Yes

F. Reject
Develop a new
name to support
extensions

9
Should the personality of the
product be the same or different
to the main brand?

Same   Different

9.1
List difference in characteristics

10
Which branded product line best
supports the product for ease of
understanding by customers?

a.
b.
c.
d.
e. None

10.2
Product/service is a new type
of activity for the brand. A
new branded product line is
required

10.1
Ensure the product name is
understandable when
described by the branded
product line description

Figure 8.3 The brand innovator's decision tree: Part 2

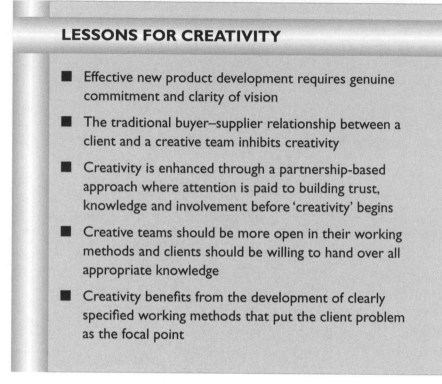

LESSONS FOR CREATIVITY

- Effective new product development requires genuine commitment and clarity of vision

- The traditional buyer–supplier relationship between a client and a creative team inhibits creativity

- Creativity is enhanced through a partnership-based approach where attention is paid to building trust, knowledge and involvement before 'creativity' begins

- Creative teams should be more open in their working methods and clients should be willing to hand over all appropriate knowledge

- Creativity benefits from the development of clearly specified working methods that put the client problem as the focal point

Note

1   Not only does NBD involve the development of new products and services it also encompasses the creation and communication of brand values, personality and image, as well as the design of brand experiences, processes and stakeholder interfaces. As such it involves the development and management of both tangible and intangible assets through holistic co-creation.

Quiksilver

Cool creativity

9

From Byron's eulogy to the oceans in *Childe Harolde's Pilgrimage*[1] to the seaside epiphany of Stephen Dedalus in James Joyce's *Portrait of the Artist as a Young Man*,[2] writers have often had a mystical relationship with the power, rhythm and sensuality of the sea. These attributes also inspire surfers to experience the adrenalin-fuelled thrill of riding waves. For dedicated surfers it represents a lifestyle outside of the mainstream with its own experiences and language. For the rest of us, the relationship is more superficial, but we can still wonder at the balance, movement, skill and daredevilry of the rider. To meet the equipment needs of surfing requires an insider perspective, which is why the culture of the largest board riding equipment company, Quiksilver, mirrors that of the sport. As Marketing Director Randy Hild says:

> These sports have a tremendous personal style. Every participant has a different routine. If you're surfing a wave, each wave is different and the way it is ridden is different. The sport is very individualistic, very free-form and very non-conventional – those things have to be in this building

[Quiksilver head office] and in what we do, otherwise we wouldn't connect with our audience.

(Interview with author dated 20 August 2003)

Collaborative culture

In the early 1970s two Australian surfers, Alan Green and John Law, were looking for a business idea that would help to fund their addiction to surfing. After a few false starts they hit upon the idea of producing surf shorts. They knew that the shorts then on offer were not really designed for the rough and tumble of surfing, so they decided to produce a robust and durable product of their own. They called the company Quiksilver. Just as Nike established itself through a close communion with athletes, so Quiksilver marketed its new shorts through the leading surfers of the day. It was a modest, hobbyist business based around word of mouth and in direct contact with its customers. Expansion came in the late seventies after business school graduate and surfer Bob McKnight and surf star Jeff Hakman bought the licence for selling Quiksilver board shorts in the USA. As well as emphasising product development, Quiksilver in the US developed the initial marketing ideas of Green and Law into a business philosophy and quickly became the dominant force among the licensees around the world. McKnight was not only passionate about surfing, he was also excited about building a brand and a business. As Hild says:

> He [McKnight] is Quiksilver. He can mix creativity with analytical ability. He is the master link on how those go together.
>
> *(Interview with author dated 20 August 2003)*

To help fuel growth there was an IPO (1986) and the entry into new but related sports: snowboarding and skateboarding. The company pushed distribution into new larger scale channels, opened its own retail outlets and developed new brands, such as Roxy, Raisins and Hawk, aimed at particular market segments. It expanded into Europe and also into Asia. And it slowly reacquired the licences around the world, so that it could control the brand better. By 2002, Quiksilver's turnover reached $700 million and its employees numbered 3000.

In the process of growing, the Quiksilver culture changed but many elements also stayed the same. It changed because of the business imperatives of shareholder accountability, the abstraction that comes with scale and the need to push the brand into more mass-market areas. However, the points of continuity are perhaps more profound. Quiksilver recognises that it is the close connection to the sports it serves that provides it with the authenticity and credibility it needs to succeed, both with the core audience and its broader fashion-based audience. For the former, the product needs to demonstrate its true sporting credentials. For the latter the appeal is coolness through association with authentic athletic performance. To achieve this connectivity Quiksilver has maintained a culture that blurs the boundaries between employee and customer. Hild says:

> If we didn't allow things to be free flowing we wouldn't get our customers. So we try to build a culture that supports that. We go back to our disciplines [surfing, snowboarding, skateboarding]; we perpetuate those disciplines; we bring in employees who understand and participate in those disciplines.
>
> *(Interview with author dated 20 August 2003)*

Skateboarder and Quiksilver Creative Director Natas Kaupas epitomises the Quiksilver brand and the approach to creativity. Natas grew up as a street, not a vertical, skater. The props for his tricks were the objects he encountered skating from his home in South Santa Monica to the beach: kerbs, benches, walls and even handrails and fire hydrants. His style derived from surfing in that it was a continuous interaction with the environment as he moved through it: a spur of the moment feeling for what might be interesting. Although skaters learn from each other, there is a strong sense of individual creativity and self-discovery in the sport. That individuality also carries through to the design of the boards. Back in the sixties, surfers had individualised their boards with spraypainting and that idea carried through into skateboarding. However, while skateboards could be hand painted by artists, many skaters including Natas, decorated the boards themselves with stickers and graffiti. When Natas became Creative Director at Quiksilver, he brought this idea of individual creativity with him and helped move the graphic design direction of the brand away from a corporate style towards one that owed more to the street. When we interviewed Natas for this book we asked him about the contradiction of trying to take the idea of individual creativity and deindividualise it by using it to define the Quiksilver brand. His answer was:

> I spent a lot of time learning about the company's personality. It's built on the riders and it's surprisingly sensitive to individuals and people. It's big hearted and the culture is inclusive and very personal. The design style is where Quiksilver is as a brand. So I kinda like the contradiction.
>
> *(Interview with author dated 6 October 2003)*

Natas' insight is that although Quiksilver is, by definition, an abstraction, it is an abstraction that focuses on individuals.

Absorption of the Quiksilver culture and of the board-riding zeitgeist is the spur for the creative process, not only for Natas, but also for the 40 or so people who work in the advertising design team. It's also the source of inspiration for Matt Anderson who is Creative Director in the product design department, where another 50 people work. Although the product design side tends to lead, the evolution of product and advertising communication usually evolves together. This is partly a result of the teams sitting and working in the same building together, but it's also about a shared passion. It helps to ensure that brand communication is tightly connected to the product and that there is no dissonance between the two. If the visual development was separate there would be a greater chance of a gap opening up. Natas says about the collaboration with Matt Anderson, 'we work in the same way and digest the influences around us and then move forward on an original path'. On the product design side this originality is fostered in a deliberate way. Each season's style is split into thirds: one third is a carry-over of the bestsellers from the previous year; one third is based on an analysis of the market and trends; one third is given over to the designers who have complete freedom to express their ideas. The first two-thirds are to ensure that the business remains consistently strong, while the last third always generates some of the future best sellers. This last slice is important, because the long-term appeal of the brand resides in its edginess; the ability to be at the forefront of board sports. Without this third, Quiksilver would be in danger of losing its core enthusiast base, which in time would reduce appeal for its mass market. This system seems to be effective, but its resilience relies on the capacity of the designers to absorb the influences of the sports.

Free-flowing creativity

Most organisations try to stimulate creativity through mechanisms such as brainstorming, research, focus groups and observational techniques. All valid tools, but limited in two respects. First, they represent subjective guesswork about the likely behaviours of an abstracted object – the customer. They reinforce the notion of us (inside the organisation) creating something for them (outside the organisation). Although these tools use the customer as a point of departure they encourage the organisation to be seller-centric, rather than buyer-centric; to focus on what the organisation does rather than the value that can be created in the life of the buyer. Second, the tools are just that, tools. They must operate within an organisational culture. Most organisations discourage continuous creativity because it is seen as the enemy of operational efficiency. So, often creativity is something that managers either try to turn on and off or they hive it off into a creative unit. The problem here is that 'creativity' becomes separated from organisational reality and the ideas generated by the tools have to fight for survival in an alien culture. They succeed, occasionally, through the commitment of passionate individuals and the subversion of corporate direction.

The Quiksilver approach to creativity is different to many organisations. It eschews most of the obvious tools and instead works on sustaining a culture of free-flowing connectivity and co-creativity. 'Free-flowing' is endemic in board sports and in the company. In the board-sports world, experimentation and freedom of expression are the keys to development. People try out new moves and do variations on existing ones. The sports then evolve through the word of mouth flow of ideas and magazines and videos. Within Quiksilver, the concept of freedom is central because it is a fast-moving market and the brand needs to be at the leading edge of the sports it serves. Quiksilver does not try to understand surfing or skateboarding trends, nor to any extent shape them, through traditional market research. Instead it is in constant and close contact with its disciplines. It has an intuitive feel for the market and the brand that is shaped by the inward–outward flow of ideas. The breaking down of the boundaries between inside and outside is the source of Quiksilver's intuition and the defining characteristic of its culture. Although this is now consciously nurtured by Quiksilver, the way of working is more a continuation of the heritage of the early Green and Law years when there were no boundaries.

Free flow in practice

Organisations often talk about the need to be close to their customers, but find it tremendously hard to do in practice. The question is, how do Quiksilver manage to achieve it? First, and most obviously, is recruitment. The people who work at Quiksilver, from the CEO down, are board-sports enthusiasts. Some are former champions in their sports, while others are just hobbyists, but all have a connecting passion with snowboarding, surfing or skating. For example, Quiksilver recognise Natas' talent and the value of his understanding of the sport. As Hild says:

> We so respect his understanding of the culture and the history [of skateboarding] … we really rely on him to tell us where we should go. Natas is in tune with the motivations of his audience, not because he has read about them in a research report, but because as he says, 'where I grew up [in Dogtown, South Santa Monica] everybody boarded and surfed. I was 4 or 5 years old when I started'.
>
> *(Interview with author dated 20 August 2003)*

Other organisations might feel uncomfortable about putting an untrained person in such a position, but for Quiksilver attitude is more important. And the company consciously provides a supportive structure with input from experienced professionals. Randy Hild says:

> The challenge is to keep an open mind … I look at everything that comes my way. We're very good listeners. The team riders and the people like Natas, they're living and breathing this kind of stuff. They're connected to the grass roots. We have great faith in these people.
>
> *(Interview with author dated 20 August 2003)*

Second, Quiksilver is a networked organisation. It maintains a network of freelance creative professionals and riders. The role of the creative professionals is to keep Quiksilver in touch with new ideas. People such as the graphic designer David Carson, who made his name with *Surfer* magazine, are used by the company to provide an external voice to the brand. Carson, like many of the other free-lancers, develops ideas outside of the Quiksilver structure but then inputs his thoughts and direction. Not all of what he produces is used, but the feeling within Quiksilver is that his input keeps the brand 'fresh and bold'. And it provides inspiration for the in-house creative teams. This is particularly important in terms of developing the advertising and design, because almost everything is developed in-house. There is no external advertising agency. Quiksilver believes that creativity is best nurtured by those directly in contact with the brand. There is also a direct connection between both the clothing and the graphic designers and the market in the form of some 240 professional riders and an army of supported enthusiasts. The riders, who are an extension of that connection to the grass roots from the early days of the business, are deeply involved in the creation of product and marketing. Quiksilver knows creativity has to meet with the approval of this audience both to ensure that it is at the forefront of trends and to maintain its authenticity. Some creative ideas are the direct result of input from riders, some are the result of dialogue and some come from negative feedback that tells the company its product isn't up to scratch or its communications don't connect. The important element of collaboration is the ability to listen. Quiksilver manage this in part by treating the riders as insiders. The language of the company reflects this: riders are part of the structure not an outside element. They appear in Quiksilver offices and connect with designers at sporting events. Their input is sought and their ideas acted upon. Hild says:

> We believe in that collaborative process; in that input from our riders. If they're not connecting with it, then our consumers probably won't connect with it …
> It's our job to listen and to adjust.
>
> *(Interview with author dated 20 August 2003)*

Third, is the importance placed on intuition. In most business contexts this is an idea that receives a veneer of support even though it may be trumpeted as an ideal. The triumph of rationality in business and the demands of accountability require people and organisations to define and implement quasi-scientific processes. Intuition is the enemy of such a philosophy. It relies on a sense or a feeling; it cannot be objectified. However it is also potentially dangerous. An overreliance on intuition can defeat creativity rather than nurture it, if group-think or individual prejudices are allowed to dominate. Quiksilver try to overcome this problem by allying the concept of intuition to open-mindedness and testing ideas against the feedback of their core audience: the riders.[3] The intuitive process seems to work because of the strength of understanding for the Quiksilver brand among the many long-serving employees. It gives them a feeling for what is right and what will work. Natas Kaupas says:

> A lot within Quiksilver happens by intuition. That's because it's a bunch of surfers – people who are unstructured, but very natural. As surfers they have to adapt to nature and the waves.
>
> *(Interview with author dated 6 October 2003)*

An example of this is the way creative work is reviewed. There is no recourse to focus groups or quantitative research. Concepts are judged by a small group of four or five people, who discuss, from an intuitive sense, which ones work. The idea of the group is that there is no formal authority and a strong sense of collaboration. Indeed, ego is something that the company is wary of in the extreme because of its potential to undermine the idea of working together. The unstructured nature of the review process seems true to the freedom-loving culture of the company and the sports, but it is in some sense a process with frameworks and rules that relies on the knowledge, understanding and interconnectedness of those involved for it to work. Quiksilver knows that if it lost its grass roots connections, it would lose its soul.

The challenge of growth

Quiksilver's ambition is to be a $1 billion company. It has to meet the needs of its shareholders and that is driving it in certain directions. It is beginning to acquire some more formal structures and processes. The company does spend more time on thinking about and discussing its strategies and it has also developed a linked mission statement. While intuition reigns, based on the immersed, long-serving employees, decisions can be made quickly without the formality of brand definitions. However, as the company grows and perhaps the core of people leave, intuition may be harder to maintain. This has certainly been the case with Nike, who found that growth required more formal statements as well as the appointment of a chief storyteller to ensure that the origins of the Nike culture were conveyed to a new generation of less sport-obsessed managers. The reliance on an intuitive feeling for the brand may also connect with the difficulty the company occasionally has working with third parties. Intuition works if people are closely connected to the brand, but when they're not, interpreting the brand becomes a guess.

The other key challenge is that growth requires pushing the brand into more diverse areas. Quiksilver has tried to limit the stretch by developing specifically targeted brands, but nonetheless the company has to market its products in more mainstream retail outlets. This creates a tension. The appeal of the product for the rider is based on its creativity and its ability to challenge preconceptions. However, the mainstream market is more conservative which means that design needs to be safer. The ability to reach both with one brand has its limits. Quiksilver has deliberately chosen not to distribute to some of the larger retailers, but if it oversteps the limit, the brand would go the way of other over-traded names. It would lose the authenticity which is at its heart.

In spite of the dangers inherent in growing the company, there are significant factors within the Quiksilver culture that should enable it to maintain its high levels of creativity. All of the core factors that can be found in the creative companies studied – trust, enjoyment, fun, valuing creativity, diversity and a desire to learn – are strongly evident within Quiksilver. In particular, there are high levels of trust and a general absence of fear. It is an informal culture where people feel free to experiment, where ideas – whatever their source – are listened to and where risk taking is part of the exhilaration of building the business. As Natas Kaupas says, 'Quiksilver works on trial and error. That's part of being a surfer.'

Conclusion

Tom Kelley (2001, pp74–5) argues in *The Art of Innovation* that passion plays a huge rule in creativity, not least in sports companies where 'they live the lifestyle they're selling'. The passion people bring to Quiksilver, whether as employees or as riders, is the source of its ability to innovate continuously both in terms of product design and marketing communications. The unity this delivers means that new ideas can and do come from everywhere both internally and externally. In this instance the boundaries of creativity are largely intuitive, but the creative process does have focus because there is such a strong understanding of the Quiksilver brand and an interconnectedness with the lifestyle of customers. The belief in intuition also encourages a very human, trust-based focus and the avoidance of the depersonalisation that so often goes with abstracted ideas derived from formalised research.

LESSONS FOR CREATIVITY

- Creativity works most effectively when there is a supportive culture; it's more important than having creative tools

- Break down the boundaries between the company and your customers; develop ideas together; co-create with the end user; encourage your employees to absorb the values and lifestyles of customers

- Recruit the right people and then support their ambitions

- Recognise the benefits of direct observation, dialogue and active listening

- Value intuition, but temper it with a questioning approach

- Allow people as much freedom as possible but balance this with accountability to objectives

- Do everything you can to stimulate passion for your business

- Have the courage to do things differently

Notes

1   Byron, in spite of his gammy leg, was a keen swimmer. When he was living in Venice he would swim from the Lido to Santa Chiara via the Grand Canal in under four hours.

2   The rhythmic narrative occurs as he watches a girl wade into the sea. It confirms his resolve to be an artist rather than a priest.

3   This reflects the work of Beth Hennessey and Teresa Amabile who argue that context specific judges are the best people to make the intuitive judgement of whether an idea is creative. See: Amabile, T.M. (1994) 'Recognizing Creativity: A Reply to Magyari-Beck' *Creativity and Innovation Management*, **3**(4): 244–5 and Hennessey, B.A. and Amabile, T.M. (1988) 'The Conditions of Creativity', in Sternberg, R.J. (ed.) *The Nature of Creativity*, Cambridge MA: Cambridge University Press.

10 Branding and Creativity

These two words – 'branding' and 'creativity' – rarely appear together in the literature on either subject. The popular view is that branding is somehow connected with logos, advertising and (in this post-no logo world) manipulation, while creativity is concerned with individual inspiration. Both viewpoints are mistaken. Branding, as we'll see in this chapter and the next, is about delivering an experience to customers and other audiences, while creativity, as we have argued throughout this book, is about a collective organisational effort aimed at differentiating a company and its products and services. That the two subjects are separate reflects the background of writers and practitioners as well as the tendency to pigeonhole both activities. Our view is that, in an organisational environment, the two are inextricably linked. The brand should define the boundaries of creativity and creativity should help to define (and sometimes extend) the brand. However, before we explore these thoughts, it is valuable to consider briefly what branding is and why it is important.

What is branding?

Branding is about people. First, the idea of the organisation and its products and services is defined and communicated outwards by the assumptions and behaviour of employees. It is their understanding of the organisational ideology and its meaning that determines actions. So for example, the way we interact with a brand like Amazon is determined by the beliefs of the individuals within the company about what it is that engages customers. This determines the operating philosophy, the software, logistics, the customer interface and after-sales back-up. The fact that all these elements are cohesively presented indicates that there is a strong internal ideology guiding people. Second, external stake-holders determine whether the brand has meaning. Branding is a concept concerned with the transformation of what a company produces into something of value for a stakeholder. Therefore a brand exists in the mind of the recipient. We are persuaded to buy a brand because it meets an unfulfilled desire or need. This is both a functional and emotional decision. Why do we prefer Puma to Nike or Diesel to Levi's? If we do, it is partly perhaps because we believe one is a better performer than the other, but mostly it is because of an emotional need to define ourselves.

For an organisation to be successful at branding it needs to be genuinely focused on buyers: to understand the motivations of customers and to communicate with them effectively. However, this process of listening and signalling is inexact and only partially controllable. The organisation may conduct market research, get good feedback from its front-line people and execute strong adver-tising and yet still fail. The reasons for this are several. As a number of the examples in this book argue, listening to customers cannot rely on market research: it is an abstraction, not reality. When we start to see numbers, we stop seeing people. This, along with the inward-looking nature of many organisations, creates marketing that is not buyer-centric, but seller-centric. Alan Mitchell (2001), author of *Right Side Up*, says that much of branding is undermined by this seller-centricity:

> The source of marketing ineffectiveness and waste, therefore, lies in its seller-centric preoccupations. Marketers say the acid test of good value is find out what your customer wants and needs and give it to them. When it comes to marketing communications, this is the one thing marketers do not do. Marketers seem to believe that the only people who do not need to practice what marketing preaches is … themselves. *(p1)*

A second limitation of market research is that customers cannot always articulate what they want, which creates particular problems in the area of innovation, as we will see in the next chapter. And, even when organisations listen well, they can still have difficulty getting their message across. Buyers have become cynical about advertising (which only records a 3% trust figure among US adults) and other corporate messaging and they are apt to listen to other voices or act like Bart Simpson who treats every marketing message with a 'good dose of protective irony' (Rushkoff 2001). As Figure 10.1 demonstrates, messages about the brand are likely to reach the customer from press comments, what friends and family say and how employees behave. When this is cohesive the buyer will have a clear picture of what is being offered by the organisation. However, if there is a lack of clear brand ideology within the organisation, the messages the buyer receives are likely to be contradictory. The result is that the buyer either ignores what is happening or is confused.

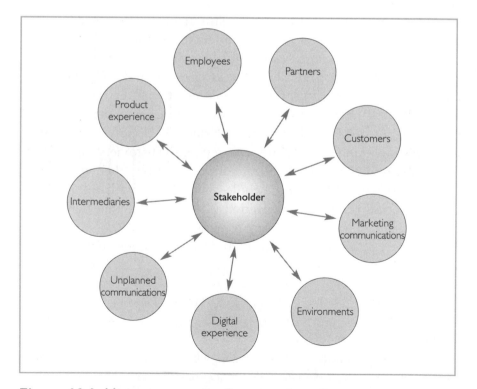

Figure 10.1 Messages can come from a variety of sources

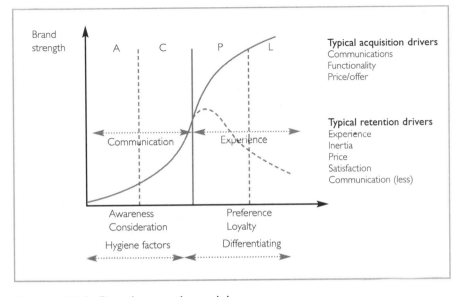

Figure 10.2 Brand strength model

Source: Ind (2003a, p22)

When the image of the brand is clear, awareness and considera-
tion indicators score highly. However, it is the repeat purchase action
of buyers over time that is truly important. This is largely defined by
experience – by the design of the product, by the interaction with
employees and the quality of service. This is the interface that matters
because, on average, 85% of a business's capitalisation is contained
within its intangible assets: in the collective knowledge and skill of
employees; the relationships with customers; the ability to innovate.
In short, the things that all connect with the brand. This is why
Coca-Cola's brand is estimated to be worth $70.5 million,
Microsoft's $65.2 billion and IBM's $51.8 billion.[1] What do these
figures mean? Essentially, they are derived from an estimate of the
future earnings attributable to the brand, discounted by the relative
strength of the brand for the consumer (see Figure 10.2). The
stronger the relationship is between the organisation and its
customer, the less the risk of the customer switching to another
brand. This is an issue of trust. The customer believes that previous
experience will be repeated – this is why some writers talk about a
brand as a 'promise of performance'.

How branding and creativity connect

Branding and creativity connect because they are both concerned with how to deliver a rewarding experience for the customer. As we have argued throughout this book, creativity is only relevant for the organisation if it is framed by boundaries. For example, it would not benefit the Quiksilver brand if the creative output of its designers lacked cohesion in terms of its range of styles and products. Nor would Tate Modern have a clear position in the minds of potential visitors if it started doing exhibitions of 12th-century Romanesque art. What branding does is to provide customer-focused boundaries that apply not just to the big strategic decisions, but also to the detailed, everyday actions of employees. If we take the example of the IceHotel in the north of Sweden, we can see this process in action. This hotel's brand is defined by two core attributes: a sense of adventure (unsurprising for a hotel made out of 30,000 tons of snow and 4000 tons of ice which melts every April); and a commitment to outstanding customer service. It seems that most often guests come for the former and end up pleasantly surprised by the latter. The sense of adventure is epitomised by a recent innovation: the construction in 2002 of an ice theatre in the form of the Shakespearean Globe Theatre, at which Shakespeare's plays are performed in Sami. Equally, the attention to service is characterised by the IceHotel guides. These employees are there to guide guests and to ensure they take advantage of the facilities of the hotel. The guides do receive intensive training so that they understand what the brand stands for, but there is also a real belief in empowerment. As Kerstin Nilsson, one of the founders, says:

> What is most important is that we tell our people that each guest is an individual and you have to treat them as an individual. We can't create rules to always say this or that. People have to have the right feeling and they have to listen.
>
> *(Interview with author dated 27 March 2003)*

These connections between customers, employees and performance are made explicit in Figure 10.3. Customers can only build relationships with an organisation through the ideas and actions of employees. Customers do want to be understood, do want expectations met and do want to be treated as individuals. This is not achiev-

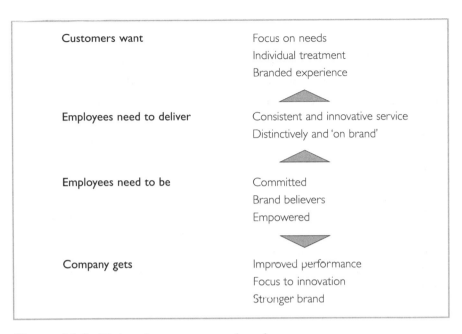

Customers want	Focus on needs
	Individual treatment
	Branded experience
Employees need to deliver	Consistent and innovative service
	Distinctively and 'on brand'
Employees need to be	Committed
	Brand believers
	Empowered
Company gets	Improved performance
	Focus to innovation
	Stronger brand

Figure 10.3 Giving the customer what they want

able with a purely system-based approach that defines behaviour. Rather it requires employee identification with the organisation and an understanding of the personal implications, or meaning, of the brand. This enables employees to work within the constraints defined by the ideology, but towards the needs of customers. The outputs of this connection are enhanced employee commitment, a focus for creativity and improved performance.[2]

While the brand sets the boundaries for creativity, both strategically and operationally, creativity should also push the boundaries. This is important because the environment in which organisations compete is dynamic and there is a constant need to differentiate in a relevant way. However, if the boundaries are defined in a creative way, such that they focus innovation rather than limit it by being dogmatic, there should be sufficient latitude to work within the boundaries. For example, Sony's 'Go Create' theme was a direct result of the company's attempt to articulate a unifying idea for itself (Gad 2003). By the late 1990s, Sony's diversifications had led to a lack of corporate cohesion. One possible solution was to restructure, but instead the company decided that the real problem lay in a lack of a clear ideology. This could have led Sony to determine a set of prescriptive ideas about itself, but instead it articulated what was at the heart of its culture: creativity. What the company realised was that people internally were motivated by the desire to express their creativity and that this had generated many of the success stories in Sony, from the Walkman to Playstation. Also Sony saw that what customers wanted were products that could enable them to fulfil their own creative aspirations. What followed was an initiative to align both existing and new products to this idea of creativity, including The Memory Stick™, which transfers information between cameras and personal computers and mobile phones and which became a tangible symbol for unification. Internally, a creativity contest was set up to encourage Sony people to work with each other across divisions. The programme was executed as if it were an external campaign, which indeed is what the theme became, thus generating one seamless idea of the Sony brand both for employees and customers. The benefit to customers in all this is that organisational creativity leads to better products, service enhancements and the joy of the new.

The joy of the new

Tim Brown of innovation consultancy IDEO says:

> It's becoming more and more clear that the behaviour of products is one of the biggest brand building things that companies have. And also the relationship between products and the brand is absolutely crucial. You have to get that connected loop to work really well … We're not necessarily doing big brand strategies for our clients, but we are trying to make sure the innovation is brand driven and that innovation drives the brand too.
>
> *(Interview with author dated 21 August 2003)*

Brown argues that the brand has always been implicit in innovation strategies but that, as companies have begun to realise the value of their brands and become self-conscious about them, the brand has become more explicit. One of the side effects of this is that more work is done when thinking about innovation, in exploring the meaning of the brand. So when Virgin, for example, looks at new opportunities, it goes back to its brand and its values (quality, value for money, innovation, competitive challenge and fun) and uses them as the benchmark. Equally, a company that has been written about elsewhere at length (Ind 2003), Patagonia, uses its values of integrity, quality, environmentalism and not being bound by convention to guide its decisions in everything it does, especially when it comes to new ideas and products. An innovation that ran counter to these values would simply not be considered. So 'new' has clear limits, which is as it should be. Customers tend to be more resistant to innovations that come from outside their range of expectations of a brand. This is because the trust the customer gives is not unbounded. While we might accept Nike rugby shirts, we would probably be more sceptical of Nike climbing equipment. We accept the former because of the heritage in other associated sports, but we are probably resistant to the latter, because climbing equipment is a highly specialised area which Nike has had no links to in the past. We might ask whether Nike could take on the climbing equipment market. It would probably find it harder than more mainstream sports equipment and it would have to approach it from the Nike brand perspective. Alternatively, we might ask whether Patagonia could be in this market. The company does make climbing clothing and in its early days it did make equipment. This suggests it would have greater credibility than Nike in this market if it chose to enter it. However, Patagonia undoubtedly would approach the climbing market very much from its environmentalist perspective.

One of the implications of this viewpoint of creating new products and services is that the brand provides a common starting point for creative processes and a means for guiding decisions and post-project evaluation. This appears constraining, but in reality it is not. Organisations that cherish creativity always have to confront the problem of the co-existence of the rational and irrational. What this means in practice is that leaders have to encourage the smooth and efficient running of operations and stimulate questioning and disruptive creativity. Generally, most leaders are more comfortable with the former. Most things in organisations, and indeed in society as a whole, are concerned with encouraging normative behaviour. The obsession with measurement is a result of this: performance measures in healthcare, academic tests, employee evaluations are all attempts to categorise the acceptable and to punish those who fail to conform. The problem with this, as Gordon MacKenzie (1998) observed:

Is that Corporate Normalcy derives from and is dedicated to past realities and past successes ... to be of optimum value to the corporate endeavour, you must invest enough individuality to counteract the pull of Corporate Gravity, but not so much that you escape the pull altogether. *(pp31, 33)*

The belief in rationality is widespread. Until recently, economic theory was dominated by the idea of the rational man. Equally, marketing, in its quest for boardroom credibility, has sought quasi-scientific justification for its methods and results. Business texts also tend to promote this idea: books pronounce there are laws, rules and systems. A linguistic analysis of Michael Porter's (1985) *Competitive Advantage*, for example, would show a strong belief in causality. Yet we know life is not like this: there is always uncertainty and doubt. One of the roles of leadership is to recognise this and to accept that uncertainty can be used to advantage – for herein lies the creative opportunity. What the organisation believes to be true can and should be challenged; new ways of doing things can and should be found. As Richard Branson says of Virgin:

As far as I'm concerned the company will never stand still. It has always been a mutable, indefinable thing.

(Cited in Whitehorn 2002, p144)

Rather more sententiously, this is the challenge that Foucault (1991b, pp32–50) defined in his definition of enlightenment. He argued that enlightenment was a way out of immaturity – a situation where the individual accepts someone else's authority. His solution to immaturity was to have the courage to know the truth; to question using reason, while respecting a reasonable system. The two thoughts are superimposed one on the other. The conclusion we might draw from Kant is that creative questioning is valuable when it is done with proper intent (to improve the way things are done) and that we should only play by the organisational rules if they are indeed reasonable.

As most organisations emphasise the importance of rationality, the goal should be to superimpose some irrationality or opportunity for creativity. For much of their time employees are asked to be highly rational individuals. Occasionally a few are let out and then asked to be creative for a short while in a brainstorming session or on an away day. Afterwards they are chained back to their desks. This is not an ideal way to encourage creativity; it cannot be turned on and off like a switch. This is not to suggest that interventions designed to unlock creativity, such as that used by Play, the Virginia-based consultancy that uses play techniques to encourage creative thinking, or Bang and Olufsen who use theatre in their new product development activities or Imagination Lab, where people use Lego bricks to help construct strategies, are not valuable. Rather it indicates that the idea of creativity needs to be absorbed into the organisational culture, if it is to have validity. Interestingly, this was one of the insights from an Imagination Lab intervention that failed. The Lab had been asked to help an aluminium firm with its strategic planning process, which seemed to be slowly grinding to a halt. However, the effectiveness of the 'serious play' organised by Imagination Lab seemed to be limited by deference to the views of the CEO and cultural factors. Whereas in other cases the Lego bricks were a spur to creativity, in this instance there was a lack of enthusiasm. The conclusion was that:

> The suppressed emotions of the team made it difficult, if not impossible, for participants to uncover new insights and ways of interacting. This finding is consistent with organisational cultural research, which indicates that organisational change is difficult when underlying values are not addressed or transformed.
>
> *(Roos et al. 2003)*

The ideal is that irrationality and creativity are incorporated into the organisational culture. The examples in this book are all designed to show the value of achieving that. However, this does require capable (and confident) leaders who can encourage a culture where freedom is encouraged. And it does require the boundary of a clear brand ideology, if anarchy is to be avoided. We have come across examples of organisations where subversive behaviour drags the organisation in different directions and away from its strategic goals and equally we have seen organisations (such as Volvo in the next chapter) where questioning and initiative subvert the accepted way of doing things, but do so in line with the brand. When the brand is clearly understood it provides the structure that allows creativity to flourish. It means that people can be genuinely empowered to use their abilities to be creative. And it means overt control mechanisms can be reduced – the brand ideology helps people understand how to set their own controls. In these environments the brand allows the rational and irrational to co-exist. The disappointment is that this approach to creativity is relatively rare. There are still a large number of organisations that favour control. Indeed, much of senior management time is spent trying to control strategy; to ensure it is implemented as planned. As Mintzberg et al. (1998) suggest:

> A great deal of what has been called strategic planning really amounts to this kind [keeping the organisation on track] of strategic control. *(p59)*

To some extent, the control a manager exerts is defined by the nature of the operating environment, but it also reflects a philosophical standpoint about trust. If we believe in the ability of the individual to make free and informed choices in line with the brand we should err on the side of freedom and in so doing capture the intellectual power of all employees. Alternatively, if we do not trust people to act responsibly, we will tend to favour a rule-based regime that defines how people should behave. The impact of these negative tendencies can be inferred from research, such as Gallup's study of US workers (2003) which found that 70% were either not engaged or actively disengaged in their jobs and a research project by tompeterscompany! among 700 business professionals in the US (live web poll conducted by www.tompeters.com 2002) which discovered that 75% of employees don't support their company's branding initiatives and that 90% don't understand how to represent the brand effectively.

Conclusion

During the Second World War there was a titanic struggle in North Africa between the soldiers of the Eighth Army (Britons, Australians, New Zealanders, Indians and South Africans) and the German Afrika Korps and the Italians that culminated in the battle of El Alamein. As described by the military historian and strategic management lecturer Stephen Bungay, the Eighth Army enjoyed, in the end, superior logistics but the Afrika Korps possessed an inspirational leader in the shape of Erwin Rommel and a doctrine that encouraged creativity within boundaries: 'The Germans had greater intellectual freedom, which they turned into greater effectiveness on the battlefield'. He goes on explain that the German Army used a system known as mission command:

The idea is that officers should understand their mission but be left free to decide for themselves how best to accomplish it. A mission consisted of a task and a purpose. Both were articulated in simple terms by the senior commander, but not specified in detail. Having understood the purpose behind their immediate task, the officers reporting to the commander were able to take decisions based on the situation as they found it – but in line with the commander's overall intentions.

(Bungay 2002, pp31, 32)

This is a clear illustration of how to balance freedom and order. In a corporate context, the order should be created by the boundaries defined by the brand (which should be closely connected to the strategy), leaving people free to express their creativity. This requires the brand to be defined in such a way that it is inspirational and engaging. And it also requires that employees understand and live the brand. If the definition remains a statement in an annual report or something pinned to a wall it cannot guide people's thinking and behaviour. It also requires trust. Trust that people will do the right thing. While the examples in this book demonstrate this, many organisations do not trust their employees. This is damaging for the individual. Employees' sense of self-worth is enhanced when there is openness, trust and participation. Lack of trust is damaging for the organisation. Research consistently shows the performance benefits of empowerment, not least because, in a world where intangible assets are so important, it makes sense to use to the full the intellectual capacity at your disposal. As Dr John Warnock, one of the founders of Adobe, says, success is, 'when good ideas come from everywhere in the organisation' (www.adobe.com).

LESSONS FOR CREATIVITY

■ Creativity works best when there is a supportive culture with a clear understanding among both leaders and employees of the brand ideology and what it means

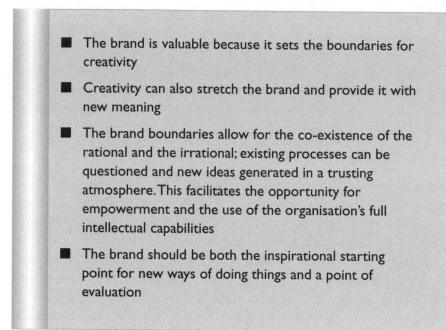

- The brand is valuable because it sets the boundaries for creativity

- Creativity can also stretch the brand and provide it with new meaning

- The brand boundaries allow for the co-existence of the rational and the irrational; existing processes can be questioned and new ideas generated in a trusting atmosphere. This facilitates the opportunity for empowerment and the use of the organisation's full intellectual capabilities

- The brand should be both the inspirational starting point for new ways of doing things and a point of evaluation

Notes

1   Interbrand brand valuations – published 4 August 2003 in *Business Week*.

2   As evidence for the benefits of this, a global study, published in September 2002 by ISR, showed that between 1999 and 2001 those organisations that had highly committed employees outperformed low commitment organisations in terms of percentage change in operating margin by more than 5 percentage points.

Driving Creativity

11

Ford's Premier Automotive Group and VW-Audi

> Being customer-driven is certainly a good thing, but if you're so customer-driven that you're merely following yesterday's trends, then, ultimately, customers won't be driving your supposedly customer-driven products.
>
> *(Flint 1997)*

One theme that has emerged throughout this book is the problem of how to use market research as an aid to creativity. Quiksilver, Funcom, Tate Modern and IDEO are all against traditional customer research as they feel it inhibits innovative thinking and weeds out good but challenging ideas. Research, they might argue is valuable in giving you an understanding of current and past behaviour, but it is problematic when trying to define a future world. As the designer, retailer and restaurateur, Terence Conran argues, people don't know what they really want until you present them with the opportunity to try it. However, while Conran and others might deride research, they are great believers in listening to and identifying with their audience. Conran's success with Habitat was because he understood the lifestyle of his customers: 'Terence was absolutely clear about who his target market was – partly because he was part of it' (Ind 1995, p148). Equally, Quiksilver employees are surfers and skaters and Funcom employees are games players.

These organisations are also adept at involving customers in the process of product development: in breaking down the boundaries between the inside and outside. This chapter looks at the uses (and abuses) of research in the automotive world. As the opening quote suggests, the particular challenge in this industry, with its long lead times and huge investments, is to try to ensure that a customer orientation is a spur to creativity not a barrier.

Inward/outward

The people who work in the automotive industry love cars. In fact they easily become obsessive about them. This is Sara Öhrvall, ex-Niche Concept Development Manager at Volvo (part of Ford's Premier Automotive Group (PAG)), talking about the culture of the company:

> The culture is so passionate you become passionate. People read all the car magazines and there are opportunities to test-drive Volvo cars and the competitors' [cars]. People talk about cars all the time. The culture is also very friendly, so people socialise a lot after working hours. Mostly they spend their free time with other Volvo people.
>
> *(Interview with author dated 13 November 2003)*

This view is echoed by PAG's Operations Director Baback Yazdani, who believes that it is essential for staff to 'live and breathe the brand everyday', although he guards against being too inward looking and strongly advocates that all members of the group be exposed to other brands and stimulants to prevent stagnation and encourage greater understanding of their world and its potential. However, for many other automotive groups this passion for the brand has remained inward looking, so hamstringing creativity.

The dominant forces in most automotive company cultures have been engineering and product development. Improving a car technically has been the source of people's passions. Such areas as design (which too often has been merely styling) and marketing (something that is done after the car is developed) have been poor relations. Yet these are the very areas that are closest to the customer and design should therefore be driving the process and marketing should be integrated with other functional areas. Generally this has not happened because of the siloisation that exists in automotive companies and the prevailing concern with engineering. However, things have begun to change. The pressure from Japanese manufacturers,[1] global over-capacity and the diminished relevance of vehicle quality as a differen-tiator have shifted the battleground. As Yazdani argues:

> Design is gaining more importance in customers' eyes as reliability and quality are almost a given these days. The differentiating factors become how the product looks and how clever it is at interfacing with the customer.
>
> *(Interview with author dated 12 August 2003)*

This is part of the reason why Ford promoted their brand-focused, design chief, J. Mays to a more senior role in 2003, so that now design has the same weight as engineering and product development. As we will see in this chapter, examples such as the Volvo Cross Country and the VW Beetle are also testament to the heightened importance of a more customer-focused approach.

The transition from inward looking to outward looking is posi-tive, because it focuses attention on the value of the product in the life of the buyer rather than what the organisation can produce. However, there is a danger that customer focus leads to a lack of courage and also lack of differentiation as car marques pursue the same interpretations of customer wants. This indicates the impor-tance of balance. Automotive companies need to use research and customer insight as a source of creative inspiration but balance this with an understanding of what is particular and unique about their brand: Volvo's interpretation of a customer insight will not be the same as BMW's or Saab's. They also need to ensure that in empha-sising design and marketing more they do not diminish the value of engineering and product development. As Yazdani says, 'a lot of creativity happens at the interfaces'. The goal should be to convert all the departments of an organisation to balancing their own contrib-ution to the brand with an understanding of the customer perspec-tive. In part, PAG achieve this through their global network of 'listening posts' that act independently from the main body of the organisation, providing concepts, new perspectives and on-the-ground knowledge of customer/cultural trends, expectations and needs. For Yazdani these creative facilities are priceless sources of knowledge and inspiration.

Brief beginnings

> Constraints are very useful things. Most creative people would say the most difficult time to be creative is when you have no constraints. Constraints can allow you to be more creative, if they are in themselves creative. I'm interested in this – how to make a better job of setting constraints. Briefs are often bad, because they're constrained in the wrong kind of way and open in the wrong kind of way ... For me, the best brief is the one that immediately opens your eyes to possibilities you haven't already seen.
>
> *Tim Brown, IDEO in interview with author*

Most projects of scale are defined by a brief. Often this is necessary to obtain management approval and budgets. However, a brief should also be an active and inspirational document that is used to direct a project and evaluate progress. It should remind people about the true meaning of the brand, the lifestyle of the customer and how a project will impact on both. This seems all too rare. Briefs tend to be inactive and rarely consulted documents, which have insufficient time spent on them. As Brown suggests, the brief is central to the creative process and should be a stimulant to new ways of thinking. This is about the proper use of research; to aid insight and to determine parameters. It is also exactly the attention that was given to the brief formation process for the Volvo Cross Country.

The V70 Cross Country, which was originally launched in 1997, was developed out of analysis and discussion. There were both market factors and internal requirements behind it. Internally, there was a requirement to build a more emotional connection between Volvo and its customers and to extend the customer base beyond the traditional Volvo buyer. Externally, although people still wanted a vehicle that supported their active and adventurous lifestyles, there was starting to be some criticism of SUVs[2] on both safety and fuel consumption grounds. The combination of these factors led to an initial discussion about developing an SUV, but there was a feeling that even a less aggressive SUV transgressed the safety aspect of the Volvo brand, so this idea was rejected. As the dialogue continued there was a recognition that the opportunity existed to interpret adventure from a Volvo perspective, which led to the idea that a new niche could be developed which was a hybrid – part station wagon, part SUV. Combining the results of the market insight and the various discussions, a brief was developed under the auspices of the marketing department. The brief contained a clear statement about the purpose of the vehicle and its relationship to Volvo's brand value proposition ('the safest and most exciting car experience'), a definition of a new 'modern family' target audience and a number of key success factors, each of which was defined from a customer perspective. Sara Öhrvall, describes the process:

> The project started with the strategy: the role of the car for the overall brand. So innovation is always done within a specific Volvo context. You start with the brand and then you say what is the role of this car in the brand and what is the position of the car in the market against other cars ... We had clear opinions about that and about who the customers would be. These were people who would appreciate the concept, even if they didn't use off-road that much. We even had the communication concept – how we would launch this car.
>
> *(Interview with author dated 13 November 2003)*

Interestingly, there are some clear parallels between the Volvo approach and J. Mays's work, before he joined Ford, on the launch of the new VW Beetle. In this case, market research was used to focus thinking about the design. The idiosyncratic shape of the original Beetle, the 'Think Small' iconic advertising campaign from the sixties and the continued presence of Beetles on the road, meant people knew the brand and were fond of it. The goal Mays set was to recreate this connection between the car and the customer. In the same way as the Volvo team thought about positioning and branding right at the outset, so did Mays with the Beetle. He and his team also used market research at the front end of the project as a source of inspiration: to try and understand the attitudes and motivations of potential buyers. Consumers were asked what they liked about the Beetle and this generated words such as 'simple', 'honest' and 'reliable'. The key words were then positioned against their opposites and a visual metaphor was developed that best matched each word. The strongest association of all was the word 'simple'. The correlating idea between this word was the shape of the circle, which became the defining idea in the brief and led to the design of the car and the inspiration for the advertising. Brooke Hodge (2002) describes the process:

> He began with an iconic car and, through careful research, identified the reasons it had become imbued with cultural and emotional associations and forecasted

how the redesign could rekindle many of the same associations and thereby increase sales for the company. *(p36)*

In both the Cross Country and the Beetle, the process of development was marketing led – in other words, the teams were trying to understand the lifestyles of potential buyers. And in both cases that understanding was used to determine a brief with a clearly defined idea based on the essence of the brand. This was the inspiration and the point of accountability for all subsequent developments in the design and marketing process. The only time that research was used to try and gauge the relevance of design rather than as a source of inspiration, it delivered a negative view that led to the temporary closure of the Cross Country project.[3] The post-project perspective at Volvo was that if a new idea does well in a focus group, then it probably means the design is boring and should be rethought.

Managing a creative team

While the brief should be the catalyst for the development process, it should also act as an integrative and inspirational force throughout the course of the project. Car development is a long-term process, involving many different disciplines and suffers from a constant pressure to compromise. For the Cross Country, one of the key parts of the process was to see if development could be speeded up, but the project still took two years and involved design, product development, engineering, quality and marketing. Each of these departments tends to be functionally independent and its members are driven by different motivations. Designers want the plaudits of their peers for the most innovative design, while engineers are interested in the most effective solution and marketers want something that will appeal to customers. As an illustrative example of what happens when the balance is wrong, a mid-1990s revamp of one Volvo model featured 1600 engineering changes, which technically produced a better car. However, the lack of buyer orientation in the process meant there was nothing to communicate to consumers. The implication is that the different disciplines need to work together rather than in their silos and they need to focus on a common vision rather than pursuing narrow agendas. The key to this is a team which is unified around the brief and understands, in-depth, the profile of the target customer. To achieve this with the Cross Country, Öhrvall created a customer environment. This was a sort of exhibition that could be laid out in several rooms and featured descriptions of consumers, pictures of their lifestyles and samples of the clothes, furniture and equipment they might own: 'we made their lives'. In another room there would be a map showing the positioning of the Cross Country relative to key competitors, alongside images of their vehicles. Finally there was a room with a clay model. The brief itself was tight, but it tried not to be prescriptive. The two core elements of the brand – 'safety' and 'excitement' – had to be adhered to, but otherwise the key success factors contained customer-focused challenges. So, for example, the brief on height which was important to enable off-road driving, to provide people with the feeling of safety they get from a higher ride and to position the vehicle as 'part way to a jeep', was not a specific objective to raise the ground clearance by a certain number of millimetres. Rather the creative challenge to the team was to give the customer the perception that the car was higher than comparable cars. To achieve this, the designers and engineers increased the ground clearance but also turned the back window upside down, so that the spoiler piece is at the bottom rather than the top. This idea makes the window, and the car, appear to be higher than they actually are.

This detailed piece of creative thinking, combined with all the other small innovations from the interior handle to steady the passenger when off-road, to the baseball-glove-like stitching in the interior, to the black wrap-around bumper are the key to differentiating the vehicle – something that, following the focus-group debacle and the enthusiasm for the product within Volvo, was pushed by many people. In fact in various acts of corporate subversion, different managers who supported the project would sometimes reallocate spare funds to support development. This informal network of advocates within the organisation provided the team with the confidence to try out new ideas. It also indicated the importance of internal communication and of building support by involving people through the customer environment rooms. However, while this support and unity were powerful, without the guiding hand of the brief it would have been difficult to keep a focus on creativity: 'the discussions would have been endless'. The brief both stimulated arguments, but it also settled them. When there was discussion about the cost of the interior, it was the importance of this element to the consumer that determined the resolution. When a feature was suggested that would enable the driver to control the ground clearance manually, there was a safety argument against it – and, because safety is at the top of brand pyramid, the idea was rejected. These different thoughts were partly the result of radically different viewpoints that people brought to the project. This encouraged people to fight for their ideas, but because competences were clearly defined, the team would tend to defer to expert opinion and to the authority of the customer-driven key success factors. This was important because brand values in themselves can sometimes seem nebulous. What does it mean in real terms to be 'innovative' or 'challenging'? With the Cross Country, attention was paid to thinking through the implications of these concepts. However, Öhrvall believes this is a major problem in most companies because people don't know how to use the brand values when it comes to product or service development, which leads to a gap between the philosophical-sounding brand values and the everyday, critical decisions in a project. She goes on to add that the values, if well thought through, are extremely useful in creating a brief around which a team can unite:

> My insight is that these people [the team assembled to work on the Cross Country] hadn't worked together before. Previously the process was sequential. In this case we worked in a team, which meant that the design people and others could explain things. Success has a lot to do with communication. The engineering people, especially, just loved being told about the consumers and how they would use the car and why they would love this feature. Because normally they would get a brief which said, do this, do that. This made them feel much more involved and made them feel more emotional about the project.
>
> *(Interview with author dated 13 November 2003)*

The sense of project ownership was also enhanced by the sense of being a group apart. Some people within Volvo were against the project from the start because it was outside the normal procedures of product development, while others were unsure about its viability. This put pressure on the team, but the threat also brought them closer together and encouraged them to be resourceful and competitive. Within the team, there was a strong belief in the goal of building a vehicle that was the best that could be achieved within the constraints of the budget and also something that was clearly differentiated by its Volvo-ness. This was helped by the positioning map of the competition, as ideas were constantly matched against the chart to check that they enhanced the differentiation. For example, the black plastic wrap-around bumper was hated in the US focus groups and various key managers lobbied to have it changed to match the colour of the car. However, the Cross Country team resisted the pressure because they argued it would move the positioning too close to the style-based jeeps. This highlights the importance when reviewing creative ideas of not only knowing what you want to achieve, but also of knowing what you don't want to be. This negative referencing is key to maintaining distance from the competition.

Creative focus

The creative focus of the Volvo Cross Country was a result of a clear understanding of the internal identity of Volvo and the meaning of the brand combined with a strong external understanding of the attitudes and lifestyles of the likely buyers. This focus is maintained throughout PAG. For J. Mays, the challenge is not only how to position a vehicle against competitors, but how to define each of the brands within the group[4] so that they can take advantage of potential synergies but also retain their clarity in the customer's mind. To achieve this, Mays employs the thinking he developed with the Beetle:

> Mays uses the tools he developed at Volkswagen-Audi – spectrum thinking[5] and cultural overlay – to shape the identity of each brand and determine which qualities or associations should be communicated by each model within the brand ... Auto show displays and marketing campaigns are built around these core values to reinforce the messages communicated by these cars.
>
> *(Hodge 2002)*

The benefit of this process, as Baback Yazdani explains it, is that each brand has a clearly defined position with clear parameters. This facilitates high levels of creativity and speeds up the design process because of the focus and accountability it delivers. Individual designers can be switched between brands to bring different and diverse perspectives without slowing down the process. This has been part of the philosophy behind Ingeni – Ford's London-based creativity centre. Formed in 2002, Ingeni's role is both to develop existing brands into new areas and to breathe new life into automotive design. To encourage this, some of the designers come from the different Ford brands, but others are furniture or fashion designers. Not only does this diversity of talent look at problems from different perspectives, it also enables Ford to develop non-automotive merchandise for its PAG brands and also for other clients. Mixing people together also allows for good ideas to be shared across different marques. This occurs partly because of being located together, but there are also links to virtual studios, such as that used by Volvo.[6] In addition PAG constantly introduces new perspectives by involving other design agencies such as Seymour Powell, as well as consultants from more diverse backgrounds including fashion and game design. Yazdani admits that such inputs are not cheap, however he firmly believes that such richness and diversity of views are key to the creative process.

The second key benefit that brand focus delivers is the ability to reject ideas, faster and more objectively. This maintains the speed of projects which is vital for people's confidence and enthusiasm and for the company's product development schedules. Mays observed the difference between the approach he experienced at VW-Audi with the way of working at Ford when he arrived. In the German methodology, the focus on one design solution comes early in the process, so that most of the time is spent developing the detail. In the traditional Ford way of working a number of ideas were developed to a more finished degree, which left very little time to execute them properly. The difference was that German designs were consequently of a higher standard. Mays has changed the way of working at Ford and now, as Yazdani notes, the gateways are there to focus processes. This also enables branding and communications work to develop alongside the vehicle design itself. The value of this is that the commercial opportunity is maintained at the forefront of the project. Mays is a strong advocate of this way of working and in the Volvo Cross Country project the brand and communication strategy were developed at the front end of the process and those responsible for advertising (including the agency) were included in the reference group.

Success is ...

As emphasised in the opening quote to this chapter the challenge is to be customer-oriented without being slavish to customer research. The new Beetle was built on an intimate understanding of customer attitudes to the old Beetle and the appeal of ideas such as simplicity and honesty. This purity could appear sterile, but it becomes emotionally engaging because the metaphor of the circle in the design and the communication is used with consistency and authenticity. The Beetle is a distinctive car with a distinctive heritage. It has charm, no pretensions and an ideal balance between form and function. Equally the team that developed the Cross Country became wary of the inputs of research, but the success of the vehicle lay in its appeal to a specific target market and the ability to extend customer expectations. As Öhrvall says:

> People without knowing it were looking for this alternative. These people thought a jeep impractical and too expensive and a normal estate car too boring. The Cross Country was on the spot: a perfect balance between design features and functional features. It looked unique but was not too outrageous.
>
> *(Interview with author dated 13 November 2003)*

Equally, in both cases the feeling for customers' future needs was met by an ability to execute, overcoming, in so doing, internal prejudices. These internal battles may have been frustrating, but the preparatory work required to build management support was a powerful stimulus to creativity. The clear success factor here was to steer the projects away from something based purely on design and towards a concept based around brand. By concentrating on the brand, the teams could demonstrate the value of the projects in terms of the impact on customer perceptions and the value to the overall business.

LESSONS FOR CREATIVITY

- The brief is a vital element in creative processes. It should stimulate creativity rather than constrain. This requires time to be spent on the brief and for it to be a living document throughout a project

- The brand should help to set the boundaries for creativity and to focus thinking on those areas most important to the development of the brand

- Intuitive understanding of customers and the role of the brand in people's lives is vital, but it is difficult to obtain this insight directly from traditional market research. Research should help the departure point for creativity, rather than being the sole checkpoint

- Genuine consumer insight is a great spur to creativity and a means of evaluation

Notes

1 In August 2003, Toyota sales in the USA were greater than Chrysler for the first time, while GM's share of the US market fell from 44.6% in 1980 to 27.8% in 2003 (source: Autodata www.motorintelligence.com).

2 Sports Utility Vehicles.

3 Volvo used focus groups in the US to get responses to a clay model. The feedback was overwhelmingly negative and the Cross Country project was killed. It was only when Subaru successfully launched their hybrid Outback that Volvo had a rethink and decided to restart the project.

4 The eight brands in the Ford portfolio are: Ford, Mercury, Lincoln, Mazda, Volvo, Land Rover, Jaguar and Aston Martin.

5 The process of matching key aspects of the car's design and its associations with a spectrum of key words.

6 www.conceptlabvolvo.com.

Conclusion

Why did you buy this book? If you were looking for insight in how to become a more creative individual, then probably you're a bit disappointed. You might find some ideas contained within the case chapters, but our argument all along has been that individual creativity can only function in the right environment. Equally, if you've been searching for those tools that business books offer up as a panacea to innovation blocks, you're also likely to be disappointed. Tools such as employee involvement groups, brainstorming sessions, prototyping and serious play are valuable mechanisms and have been well explained by such organisations as IDEO, Play and Imagination Lab. Interesting though these tools are, the world does not need another book on them. In any case, our belief is that tools are only effective in a supportive culture. You can easily transport some of the methods used by IDEO, but you cannot easily replicate their people and their ideology. Our simple conclusion is that to enhance creativity, you have to work on the culture. You have to foster the right kind of leadership, recruit and develop the right kind of people and encourage the right culture: one based on empowerment, confidence and trust. The downside to this is that we do not provide a quick fix. You can easily implement some of the ideas we suggest but cultural transformation takes time and commitment. This might be off-putting, but unless you're willing to work on developing a creative culture, the impact of individual creativity and creativity tools will always be constrained and you will not deliver sustained innovation. This has been the goal of this book: to provide insight and inspiration about creativity and to provide ideas about what you can do to build a culture where creativity is not a department or an occasional exercise but a living, breathing, integral part of your organisation. The virtue of this is that it provides the organisation with a real competitive advantage by differentiating products and services and it rewards employees by creating an energetic, inspiring place to work. By way of conclusion this chapter summarises the key ingredients for creating such a culture.

Trust

Several of the organisations featured in this book are Swedish: Volvo, the IceHotel and Moderna Museet. This is not serendipity. According to the Innovation Scoreboard, published by the European Commission, Sweden is the number one country in the world for innovation.[1] Interestingly, the countries that score highly in this study are generally Northern European, Protestant countries and the ones that perform below the norm are Southern European, Catholic countries. This may be connected to the fact that Protestant cultures are what Hampden-Turner and Trompenaars (2000) call 'universalist': focused on sameness and similarity where laws and rules are applied in a universal way. The benefits of universalism are high trust societies and high levels of social capital. This is born out by data on interpersonal trust, which again ranks Sweden (along with Norway and Denmark) at the top (Inglehart 2000). Some interesting insights derive from these connections. First, we might assume that creativity would thrive in southern European particularist cultures where there is less pressure to conform. This may be true at the individual level but, when it comes to the organisational level, creativity seems to thrive in universalist cultures where there are clearer rules and where diversity is celebrated. Second, there is an interesting connection between high levels of trust in society and innovation. Third, Sweden also scores the highest in terms of a self-expression dimension that encompasses some important ingredients that are also valuable creativity stimulants:

postmaterialist values, trust, tolerance, political activism and subjective well-being (Inglehart 2000). What we can see in Swedish society then is social capital:

> An instantiated set of informal values or norms shared among members of a group that permits them to cooperate with one another. If members of the group come to expect that others will behave reliably and honestly, then they will come to trust one another. Trust acts like a lubricant that makes any group or organisation run more efficiently.
>
> *(Fukuyama 2000)*

What we see at the national level can also be seen within the Swedish organisations in this book: they tend to be participative and non-hierarchical and advocates of genuine empowerment. Their leaders have to earn trust and respect and can be expected to be questioned by employees. But equally, once trust is established, employees focus on working together as a team. Egotism is not encouraged. This way of working is not limited to Swedish companies – we can see the same sort of traits in companies such as Quiksilver and IDEO – but what can be observed is that the overall cultural context encourages it. A Swedish manager would struggle to impose a system on an organisation if it had not been discussed beforehand and instituting a bureaucratic structure would probably be met with acts of subversion. The implication is that leaders have to trust employees and use a mentoring style of leadership rather than trying to direct and overly control people. When this works well, its value is that creativity is encouraged – employees are given the opportunity to express their ideas. Similarly, once leaders have established their credibility by demonstrating professional competence and delivering on promises made, employees can be highly supportive. Key to this mutual trust is a requirement for clarity. Leaders – ideally with input from employees – need to articulate a clear vision and employees need to understand the implication of the vision for their day-to-day work. As Lars Nittve points out, this mutual trust gives people the confidence to try new things and makes them more accepting of well-intentioned failure. This helps people feel that they can fulfil their potential rather than accepting the disappointing reality of most organisations where employees feel that their dreams are never realised.

Focus

The organisations we interviewed described their approach to creativity in different terms, but they all recognised the importance of boundaries or constraints, which they sometimes talked about in terms of the brand or values. This seems like a counter-intuitive idea, because a commonly held assumption is that creativity is about freedom. It is not. It is about balancing freedom and order. Creativity without order is anarchy. The purpose of creativity is to help an organisation to meet its goals. It does this by working within the constraints of the organisational strategy and the parameters defined by the brand. Thus if a brand is defined in terms of 'safety' and 'excitement' (as we saw with Volvo), the meaning behind those words should dictate the scope of creativity. In this instance, a suggestion to innovate in an unsafe way would be inappropriate, as would a design that failed to deliver the idea of excitement. For this reason, we believe it to be vital that brands are defined in a credible way. There should always be some forward movement in a brand. An aspirational quality that stretches the organisation. However, if the definition is too aspirational, people will see it as fanciful and reject it as wishful thinking. Thus, aspiration must be balanced by a feeling of what is true for the organisation. Some aspects of the definition should reinforce what is valuable and strong. This helps to ensure that when people are innovating, their sense of the brand comes to the fore. We can see the evidence for this in the Cross Country project, where the brand provided the bedrock for the project, while the company tackled new challenges, such as creating a new automotive segment and targeting a new audience for the Volvo brand.

To appreciate the value of boundaries (or whatever the organisation calls them) all we have to do is imagine managing a project where they are removed. How now do we define anything but a prescriptive brief that instructs people rather than involves them? How do we make sure that what we do has any strategic relevance to the organisation? How do we get team members to focus their attention? How do we evaluate what people produce and know which ideas to reject? The only solution is defining a dictatorial process based on a subjective idea of what will work – not the best way to stimulate creativity. The way out of this trap is to ensure that the boundaries are clear and that people absorb them through the example of leaders living and talking about them, through the experience of using them in everyday work and through relentless communication. This then allows employees the freedom to experiment within the boundaries on an ongoing basis. They don't have to wait for the monthly creativity session – they can question and participate all the time. The organisation begins to capture the potential of its collective intellectual capacity. Employees enjoy having the opportunity to express their creativity. All it requires is to set the boundaries.

Listen and learn

How do organisations listen? The obvious way is through market research, but we have seen the limitations of research as a tool when dealing with creativity. It is very hard for people to imagine a future-based idea and place it in their own lives. And much as organisations are keen to reduce risk, research of this kind simply undermines opportunities. However, research can be used to inspire people as to possibilities and it can stimulate interesting connections by creating a living profile of likely buyers or defining a context for products in a future world. The scenario organisation, Global Business Network (GBN), argues:

> Competitive advantage is rooted consequently in understanding your marketplace. In the years ahead, we believe the new terrain for business will introduce an additional imperative for continued success, namely, *adaptive advantage*, which is rooted in understanding the world. Adaptive advantage will come to those best able to adapt swiftly and wisely to the changing external environment.
>
> *(Kelly et al. 2002, p302)*

GBN believes that one of the keys to this understanding is thinking from the outside in. This is similar to Alan Mitchell's argument about the prevalence of seller-centric organisations and the value of buyer-centricity. There is always a tendency to think from the point of view of what we, in the organisation, can do with the resources we have. Of course, this is important, but it is at the point of interaction with the buyer that value is created. This suggests the organisation has to focus consciously on the life of the buyer and the world in which they live. To take some of the examples in this book, the best way of achieving this is to break down the barriers between the organisation and its external audiences. As we saw with Quiksilver, an organisation that truly connects with its audience by involving them in the business and co-creating new products with them, reduces risk and gains adaptive advantage. This co-creation idea also implies that the people within the organisation should be migrating in the opposite direction. That is why Volvo encourage people to test drive other cars, Quiksilver recruit athletes and encourage employees to surf and skate and IDEO develop new product ideas themselves and take part in design challenges. Employees in these organisations are not racing home at the end of the day to watch television, they're out there connecting with the environment in which they work. By encouraging this connectivity an organisation can create an integrated network that encompasses people both inside and outside the business. And providing there are questioning voices and group-think is avoided, this is a much better way of understanding the future: rather than the abstraction of market research, managers and employees experience the real world where their products and services are bought. This is the business equivalent of Gonzo, which was made famous by the writer, Hunter S. Thompson, who immersed himself in his stories and books, rather than trying to objectively observe and analyse.[2]

As well as connecting with the outside it is then important that knowledge is shared. Innovations are often the result of connecting knowledge internally. Most organisations have explicit mechanisms for encouraging this sharing, but it is surprising how often these connections are missed. The primary factor here is the siloisation that is prevalent in organisations of any size. As Lou Gerstner (2002), former head of IBM, writes:

> One of the most surprising (and depressing) things I have learned about large organizations is the extent to which individual parts of an enterprise behave in an unsupportive and competitive way toward other parts of an organization. It exists everywhere. (p249)

Overcoming these internal barriers requires a unifying vision, and also structures and measurement systems that encourage horizontal communication and cooperation. The tendency of employees will be to identify with their most immediate unit rather than the corporate whole.[3] The challenge is to ensure that the corporate brand also has meaning. This facilitates the more informal, intuitive type of learning that we have seen in many of the organisations cited in this book. Ideas are shared in Quiksilver, Funcom and Moderna Museet because people understand the overall corporate direction and share with each other a community of interest. It could be argued that this community is easy to achieve in such business areas as art, games and sports where people are very passionate, but it does also work in other, more prosaic, industries. If employees are properly empowered they will react to their experience and then share it with others. At the operational level, an example of this is Xerox photocopier engineers. At the official level there is a handbook that instructs the engineers how to deal with problems. This explicit knowledge is useful to a certain extent, but in a study of what engineers actually do, it is the informal networking that proves to be more powerful. Engineers learn about problems related to specific machines as they work and through talking to customers. This knowledge then becomes embedded through the casual day-to-day conversations that take place when engineers meet for coffee or in the office. Sensibly Xerox have recognised the reality of how the engineers work and have built a knowledge system, called Eureka, that seeks to encourage the sharing of ideas.

> Executives who want to identify and foster best practices must pay very close attention to the practices as they occur in reality rather than as they are represented in documentation or process designs. Otherwise, they will miss the tacit knowledge produced in improvisation, shared through story-telling, and embedded in the communities that form around those activities.
>
> *(Brown and Duguid 2000, p79)*

Execution

Effective teams are the basis of creativity. However, simply lumping people together and telling them to be creative, tends not to be very productive. As Tate Modern, Funcom and Volvo all demonstrate, teams need to be carefully constructed in terms of personnel, given clear lines of accountability and supported by leaders. There is no magic formula for getting this right, but emotional intelligence is vital to the construction and guidance of teams. Leaders need to know when to direct, when to mentor and when to leave alone. They have to develop a feeling for when the group is working well and when it is not. They also need to think about the following balances:

- team members should have high levels of professional competence to gain the respect of their colleagues, but they should not be egotistical

- diversity of background is valuable in bringing different perspectives to a problem, but there should also be a unifying ideology

- there should be sufficient members of a team to best tackle the problem at hand without creating a group that is too unwieldy and where decision making is difficult

- there must be trust within the group and towards leadership but there should also be a challenge that stretches people's abilities

- there must be clearly defined boundaries, but within those boundaries there should be freedom.

Over and above these requirements, the accountability of the team needs to be defined. The challenge for the team needs to be genuine and important and the outputs actioned. Without rapid feedback and support from management, disillusion will soon set in. People will begin to feel that the team's task is a charade and that it has little relevance to the organisation. This suggests that if teams are to function optimally, openness and honesty are vital components of the organisational culture.

What we can also observe is that creativity is important in the detail as well as in the big idea. There seems something heroic about the individual or the team that conceives, in an original moment of inspiration, something revolutionary. However, ideas are rarely implemented as originally conceived. They have to be worked out and adapted to the competencies of the organisation and the needs of buyers. We saw this need for granular creativity particularly in the cases of Funcom and Aardman, but also Tate Modern and Volvo. An original idea can die in the process of development or fail to realise its potential, but the opposite can also happen in that it can be enhanced. The latter requires the creative leader to define and communicate the vision for the idea and then allow people the freedom to use their own creativity to interpret it. This has to be a managed process and the creative leader has to be a good editor of the ideas of others and have the humility to know when an original idea has been improved.

People

The title of this book, *Inspiration,* was only arrived at after much discussion. Shouldn't the word 'creative' be in the title or perhaps 'innovation'? In the end our preference for 'inspiration' was founded on the principle that creativity is for, and about, people. That may seem an obvious statement, but in analysing creative processes, it's all too easy to forget. What we want to emphasise is that organisational creativity is designed to create value by providing something that meets the needs and aspirations of buyers. Creativity should bring joy, beauty and inspiration to the world. And if we stop to think for a minute about watching a Wallace and Gromit film, experiencing the collections of the Tate Modern, visiting the IceHotel, driving a VW Beetle, listening to a Glyndebourne opera or playing a Funcom game we can see how creativity achieves this. It offers us new experiences and rewards our need for personal fulfilment.

Equally within the organisation, inspiration is a vital element. Leaders should have the ability to inspire colleagues and employees by articulating and communicating a clear, unifying vision. Also they should increase the potential for creativity by recruiting people who have a positive attitude and by nurturing their potential through intrinsic rewards. For the individual employee, the role is part recipient and part giver. The employee should hope to inspire others and to forge creative links across the organisation and upwards. Some might argue this is difficult to achieve in their organisation but, as the philosopher Karl Popper (2002) argues about institutions, they cannot improve themselves. With freedom of action comes the responsibility to improve the world. Employees need to seize the opportunity to shape their workplaces. Similarly, the employee also hopes to be inspired by leaders and colleagues. Mostly people join organisations because they identify with an ideology. Over time, as their aspirations are unrealised, they become disappointed. This should not be an inevitable journey. Employees want to be inspired and want to use their creativity. This occurs most clearly in the people-focused, high-energy and trusting organisational cultures featured in this book. It's also worth stressing that these cultures are more fulfilling and fun.

Notes

1   2001 Innovation Scoreboard – the US and Japan also perform above average.

2   Gonzo journalism is the personal and subjective form of writing that Hunter S. Thompson advocates, where the writer is an active participant in the narrative.

3   Research by Onno Maathias (PhD 1999 'Corporate Branding', Erasmus University, Rotterdam) shows that employees identify with their immediate business unit more strongly than with the organisation as a whole.

Bibliography

Allen, Woody (1975) *Without Feathers*. London: Random House.

Amabile, T. (2001) 'How to kill creativity', in Henry, J. (ed.) *Creative Management*. London: Sage, pp4–10.

Amabile, T.M. and Conti, R. (1994) 'Environmental determinants of work motivation, creativity and innovation: The case of R&D downsizing', Paper presented at the Technological Oversights and Foresights Conference, Stern School of Business, New York.

Amabile, T.M., Conti, R., Coon, H., Lazenby, J. and Herron, M. (1996) 'Assessing the work environment for creativity', *Academy of Management Journal*, **30**(5): 1154–84.

Bar-On, R. (2000) 'Emotional and Social Intelligence: Insights from the Emotional Quotient Inventory', in R. Bar-On and J.D.A. Parker (eds) *Handbook of Emotional Intelligence*. San Francisco: Jossey Bass, pp363–88.

Belbin, R.M. (1993) *Management Teams. Why They Succeed or Fail*. Oxford: Butterworth Heinemann.

Blois, K. (1999) 'Trust in business to business relationships: an evaluation of its status', *Journal of Management Studies*, March, **36**(2): 197–215.

Bloom, Harold (2001) *How to Read and Why*. London: Fourth Estate, p21.

Brown, John Seeley and Duguid, Paul 'Balancing act: how to capture knowledge without killing it'. *Harvard Business Review*. May–June 2000, p79.

Bungay, Stephen (2002) *Alamein*. London: Aurum Press.

Byron, Lord George Gordon (1975[1812]) 'Childe Harolde's Pilgrimage' in John D. Jump (ed.) *Childe Harolde's Pilgrimage and Other Romantic Poems*. London: J.M. Dent & Sons.

Chan Kim, W. and Mauborgne, R. (2003) 'Fair process: managing in the knowledge economy', *Harvard Business Review*, **81**(1): 127–36.

Collins, Jim (2001) *Good to Great*. London: Random House Business Books.

Cringely, Robert, X. (1996) *Accidental Empires*. London: Penguin.

Csikszentmihalyi, Milhaly (1997) *Creativity Flow and the Psychology of Discovery and Invention*. New York: Harper Perennial.

Cullen, J. Johnson, J. and Sakano, T. (2000) 'Success through commitment and trust: the soft side of strategic alliance management', *Journal of World Business,* **35**(3): 223–40.

de Bono, Edward (1967) *New Think: The Use of Lateral Thinking in the Generation of New Ideas.* New York: Basic Books.

de Botton, Alain (2002) *The Art of Travel.* London: Hamish Hamilton.

Ellsberg Daniel (2002) *Secrets: A Memoir of Vietnam and the Pentagon Papers.* New York: Viking.

Emmerling, R. and Goleman, D. (2003) 'Emotional Intelligence: issues and common misunderstandings'. Consortium for Research on Emotional Intelligence in Organizations.

Flint, J. (1997) 'Chrysler', *Forbes Magazine,* January 13: 84.

Ford, C. and Gioia, D. (2000) 'Factors influencing creativity in the domain of managerial decision making', *Journal of Management,* **26**(4): 705–32.

Foucault, M. (1991a) 'Nietzche, Genealogy, History', in Rabinow, P. (ed.) *The Foucault Reader* (trans. Catherine Porter). London: Penguin.

Foucault, M. (1991b) 'What is Enlightenment?', in Rabinow, P. (ed.) *The Foucault Reader* (trans. Catherine Porter). London: Penguin.

Fukuyama, F. (2000) 'Social capital' in Harrison, Lawrence and Huntington, Samuel P. (eds) *Culture Matters: How Values Shape Human Progress.* New York: Basic Books.

Fukuyama, F. (2001) 'Technology, networks and social capital', in Henry, J. (ed.) *Creative Management.* London: Sage, pp225–38.

Gad, Thomas (2003) 'Leadership Branding', in Nicholas Ind (ed.) *Beyond Branding.* London: Kogan Page.

Gallup (2003) 'Measuring and Improving Employee Engagement', www.gallup.com.

Gerstner, Louis V. (2002) *Who Say Elephants Can´t Dance?* p249, New York: Harper Business.

Gladwell, Malcolm (2001) *The Tipping Point: How Little Things Can Make a Big Difference.* London: Abacus.

Golding, William (1997[1954]) *Lord of the Flies.* London: Faber and Faber.

Goleman, D. (1995) *Emotional Intelligence: Why it Can Matter More Than IQ.* London: Bloomsbury..

Goleman, D. (2001) 'What makes a leader', in Henry, J. (ed.) *Creative Management.* London: Sage, pp127–39.

Hampden-Turner, Charles and Trompenaars, Fons (2000) *Building Cross-cultural Competence: How to Create Wealth from Conflicting Values.* Chichester: John Wiley and Sons.

Handy, C. (2001) 'The citizen company', in Henry, J. (ed.) *Creative Management.* London: Sage, pp240–51.

Henry, J. (2001a) *Creativity and Perception in Management*. London: Sage.

Henry, J. (2001b) *Creative Management*. London: Sage.

Herzberg, F. (2003) 'One more time: how do you motivate employees?', *Harvard Business Review*, January, **81**(1).

Hodge, Brooke (2002) 'Desiring design: J. Mays's innovative approach', in *Retrofuturism, The Museum of Contemporary Art*. New York: Los Angeles and Universal Publishing.

Ind, Nicholas (1995) *Terence Conran – the Authorized Biography*. London: Sidgwick and Jackson.

Ind, Nicholas (2003) *Living the Brand: How to Transform every Member of your Organization into a Brand Champion*, 2nd edn. London: Kogan Page.

Inglehart, Ronald (2000) 'Culture and democracy', in Harrison, Lawrence and Huntington, Samuel P. (eds) *Culture Matters: How Values Shape Human Progress*. New York: Basic Books.

Janis, I.L. (1982) *Group Think*. Boston: Houghton Mifflin.

Joyce, James (1977[1916]) *Portrait of the Artist as a Young Man*. St. Albans: Panther Books.

Jung, C.G. (1993) *The Basic Writings of C.G. Jung*, V. Staube de Laszlo (ed.). New York: The Modern Library.

Kelley, Tom with Littman, Jonathan (2001) *The Art of Innovation: Lessons in Creativity from IDEO, America's Leading Design Firm*. New York: Currency Doubleday.

Kelly, Eamonn, Leyden, Peter and GBN (2002) *What's Next? Exploring the New Terrain for Business*. Cambridge: Perseus Books.

King, N. and Anderson, N. (1990) 'Innovation and creativity in working groups', in West, M.A. and Farr, J.L. (eds) *Innovation and Creativity at Work*. Chichester: Wiley, pp81–100.

King, Stephen (1973) *Developing New Brands*. London: JWT.

Koestenbaum, Peter and Block, Peter (2001) *Freedom and Accountability at Work: Applying Philosophic Insights to the Real World*. San Francisco: Jossey Bass Pfeiffer.

MacKenzie, Gordon (1998) *Orbiting the Giant Hairball*. New York: Viking Penguin.

Manville, Brook and Ober, Josiah (2003) 'Beyond empowerment: building a company of citizens', *Harvard Business Review*, **81**(1).

Maslow, Abraham (1998) *Maslow on Management*. Chichester: John Wiley & Sons.

Mayer, J.D. and Salovey, P. (1997) 'What is Emotional Intelligence?', in P. Salovey and D. Sluyten (eds) *Emotional Development and Emotional Intelligence: Implications for Educators*. New York: Basic Books, pp3–34.

Mintzberg, H., Ahlstrand, B. and Lampel, J. (1998) *Strategy Safari*. Harlow: Pearson Education.

Mitchell, Alan (2001) *Right Side Up: Building Brands in the Age of the Organised Consumer*. London: HarperCollins Business.

Mitchell, Alan (2003) 'Beyond Brand Narcissism', in Nicholas Ind (ed.) *Beyond Branding*. London: Kogan Page.

Moore, John (2003) 'Authenticity', in Nicholas Ind (ed.) *Beyond Branding*. London: Kogan Page.

Morgan, G. (1997) *Imaginization. New Mindsets for Seeing, Organizing, and Managing*. London: Sage.

Morse, Gardiner (2003) 'Why we misread motives', *Harvard Business Review*, **81**(1).

Nicholson, C., Compeau, L. and Sethi, R. (2001) 'The role of interpersonal liking in building trust in long-term channel relationships', *Journal of the Academy of Marketing Science*, **29**(10): 3–15.

Orwell, George (1981) *A Collection of Essays*. New York: Harvest Books.

Popper, Karl (2002[1945]) *The Open Society and its Enemies*. London: Routledge.

Porter, Michael (1985) *Competitive Advantage: Creating and Sustaining Superior Performance*. New York: The Free Press.

Rickards, T. (1988) *Creativity at Work*. Aldershot: Gower.

Roos, Johan, Victor, Bart and Statler Matt (2003) 'Playing seriously with strategy', Working Paper 2003–2a, Imagination Lab.

Rushkoff, Douglas (2001) 'The pursuit of cool' at www.rushkoff.com.

Sen, Amartya (1999) *Development as Freedom*. New York: Anchor Books.

Sethi, R., Smith, D. and Park, C.W. (2002) 'How to kill a team's creativity', *Harvard Business Review*, August, **80**(8): 16–18.

Simons, R. (1995) 'Control in an age of empowerment', *Harvard Business Review*, March–April: 80–8.

Thompson, L. and Brajkovich, L.F. (2003) 'Improving the creativity of organizational work groups', *Academy of Management Executive*, **17**(1): 96–112.

Whitehorn, Will (2002) 'A brand without limits', in Schmidt, K. and Ludlow, W.C. *Inclusive Branding*. Basingstoke: Palgrave Macmillan.

Index

O

Öhrvall S 144, 147, 149–53
Organisational structures
   Balanced 22–7
   Citizen 22–6
   Flat 21–6
   Hierarchical 21–6, 91
   Network 22–6, 46, 78–87, 145–8
   Self-organised 23–7, 46–9
   Supportive 11, 22–5, 55, 62–71, 75,
     81–7
Orwell G 41
Ownership
   Collective 37, 60–71, 75–87
   Project 150–3

P

Park Avenue Productions 102–5
Park N 61–2, 68
Passion 128, 144
Patagonia 137
Pauling 40, 50
People 163–4
Pickard D 89–101
Pink Roccade 14
Play 139, 155
Playstation 136
Popper 163
Porsche 37
Porter M 138
Post Office 37
Premier Automotive Group 14, 23, 47,
   50–3, 143–53
Project
   Creative 37, 107–18
   Documentation 113–18
Promises, delivery of 43–58
Puma 131

Q

Quiksilver 15, 48, 51, 53, 62, 119–29, 143,
   157, 160–3

R

Rationality 138–41
Recruitment 13–16, 31, 55, 66, 92–3, 163
Relationships
   Building trust-based 104, 111–16
   Business-to-business 107

Collaborative 29–39, 81–7
Creative 11–27
Customer 124–9, 134, 142
Equitable 33, 107–9
External 36–9, 62
Ideal 109–10
Internal 14–16, 42–58, 63–71, 81–7
Process and structure, value of 114
Tensions 107–18
Research, value of 91, 123, 126, 131–2,
   143–7, 153
Respect 97–101
Risk 1–4, 11–36, 43–63, 81–7
Rocky the Flying Rooster 59–60
Roles
   Specialisation 21
   Understanding of 105–6, 111–18
Rommel E 140
Rushkoff 132

S

Second World War 140–1
Seller-centric 131, 159
Sen A 73
Sensitivity 98–9
Sethi et al. 20
Shakespeare W 134
Siemens N 54
Simpson B 132
Sinclair C 12
Skateboarders 121–9
Skills 14–15
Smart car 12
Sony 135–6
Speed 104
Sproxton D 61–71
Stark P 28
Stress 19
Surfing 119–29
SUV 146
Swatch 12
Sweden 156–7

T

Tate Modern 76, 89–101, 134, 143, 161–9
Teams
   Autonomy in 46–58, 75–87
   Building of 11–27
   Conflict in 67–8, 75–87